Praise for *Emotional Detox for Anxiety*

"*Emotional Detox for Anxiety* points to something that's far more important than how we think and feel—how we think and feel about how we think and feel. Seeing our reactions to our experiences in a new light is key to change. This book shows you how to do just that!"
—Amy Johnson, PhD, author of *The Little Book of Big Change: The No-Willpower Approach to Breaking Any Habit*

"*Emotional Detox for Anxiety* gives you the tools to take action to live a life of joy and ease. I expect Sherianna's renowned C.L.E.A.N.S.E. method will make a huge impact on the way we treat, understand, and help people with anxiety."
—Elizabeth Hamilton-Guarino, founder and CEO of The Best Ever You Network and author of *Percolate: Let Your Best Self Filter Through*

"If you struggle with anxiety and uncontrollable reactions to emotional triggers, Sherianna Boyle's book, *Emotional Detox for Anxiety*, is a must-read. She shares her powerful C.L.E.A.N.S.E. process, which is seven steps to releasing anxiety and energizing joy. These steps encourage you to process your feelings so you can create an inner healing space of personal nourishment, freedom, and guidance. You will free yourself from repetitive toxic emotions, release judgments fueled by fear, and learn to increase your physical, mental, and spiritual energy."
—Mal Duane, author of *Broken Open: Embracing Heartache and Betrayal As Gateways to Unconditional Love*

"As someone who once struggled with panic attacks, I know firsthand the poisonous impact anxiety can have on a person's life. If your anxiety is keeping you locked in fear, avoidance, analysis paralysis, or self-criticism, Sherianna Boyle's *Emotional Detox for Anxiety* is a remedy....When faced with life's challenges, we often want to run from our emotions. Sherianna teaches the reader how to understand and embrace emotions without judgment, process them, and ultimately experience genuine peace and joy. Some of my personal favorite gems in *Emotional Detox for Anxiety* are the 'allow statements.' What a gift Sherianna has given the world with this book."
—Dr. Colleen Georges, coach, TEDx speaker, and author of *RESCRIPT the Story You're Telling Yourself*

Praise for *Emotional Detox for Anxiety*

"In her powerful new book, *Emotional Detox for Anxiety*, Sherianna Boyle shows us how we can emotionally detox our stress and anxieties with her groundbreaking C.L.E.A.N.S.E. method. She expertly applies her proven emotional detox tools to anxiety so that we can go from simply managing anxiety to healing it. Sherianna reminds us that we have the inner power to release our anxiety and create a purposeful, happy, and joy-filled life. A must-read for anyone who is struggling with anxiety, stress, and emotional overwhelm."

—Dr. Debra Reble, intuitive psychologist, bestselling author of *Soul-Hearted Living*, and creator of the Anxiety Rx: Balm for the Soul program

"Richly engaging and wise, Sherianna is one of my favorite wellness authors, and *Emotional Detox for Anxiety* is practical and transformational. Sherianna leads the reader with seven steps to look inward, release harmful thoughts, and move into a natural state of inner joy. This well-researched book is on my Kind Yoga Mindfulness and Meditation school's self-care reading list for students. I highly recommend it!"

—Diane Kovanda, MEd, coauthor of *Good Night Yoga* and founder and director of Kind Yoga Mindfulness and Meditation school (KindYoga.com)

"Activate more joy in your life. *Emotional Detox for Anxiety* guides you through the powerful C.L.E.A.N.S.E. method and offers a supportive framework to help you detox from the worries, stress, and self-doubt that are sabotaging your joy and inner peace. Sherianna is a beacon of light for those struggling with anxiety!"

—Linda Joy, inspirista, publisher of *Aspire Magazine*, and founder of InspiredLivingUniversity.com

EMOTIONAL DETOX FOR ANXIETY

7 STEPS TO RELEASE ANXIETY AND ENERGIZE JOY

SHERIANNA BOYLE, MED, CAGS
Author of *Emotional Detox*

ADAMS MEDIA
NEW YORK LONDON TORONTO SYDNEY NEW DELHI

Adams Media
An Imprint of Simon & Schuster, Inc.
57 Littlefield Street
Avon, Massachusetts 02322

First Adams Media trade paperback edition December 2019

ADAMS MEDIA and colophon are trademarks of Simon & Schuster.

For information about special discounts for bulk purchases, please contact Simon & Schuster Special Sales at 1-866-506-1949 or business@simonandschuster.com.

The Simon & Schuster Speakers Bureau can bring authors to your live event. For more information or to book an event contact the Simon & Schuster Speakers Bureau at 1-866-248-3049 or visit our website at www.simonspeakers.com.

Manufactured in the United States of America

10 9 8 7 6 5 4 3 2 1

Library of Congress Cataloging-in-Publication Data has been applied for.

ISBN 978-1-5072-1210-3
ISBN 978-1-5072-1211-0 (ebook)

DEDICATION

To my husband, Kiernan Boyle: After twenty-one years of marriage and one close call to ending it all, you chose to heal and by doing so, you gave me a chance to heal as well.

Thank you for rising above, for your unconditional love, and for your unwavering strength and support. Most of all thank you for being my best friend. Cheers to you (and me!) for completing a long chapter of resisting pain and for writing a new one of emotional connection. I love ya, babe.

Thank you to our girls: Megan, you make me proud beyond belief. Keep drawing; you have a gift for stimulating feeling. Mikayla, I'm grateful for your depth, wisdom, and inspiration; the world is your oyster. Makenzie, thank you for our nightly prayers, your humor, and your smile; you are my little healer.

Thank you to my beautiful mama, Judy Zradi, for never shaming my emotions, for giving me the space to breathe, and for always being proud of me. Also, thank you, Mom, for always encouraging me to do what I felt was right rather than follow what other people thought. Thanks to my father, Larry Zradi, for telling me you love me at the end of every phone call. I know there were many years when I did not allow myself to feel all my emotions around you and I am so grateful that is no longer the case.

Thank you to my editor, Alice Peck, for doing an incredible job sorting through this new way of thinking and addressing anxiety. I am fortunate to have your influence on this project. To Karen Cooper and the team at Adams Media, a division of Simon & Schuster, thank you for continuing to nurture the Emotional Detox project and vision.

I also want to thank my clients. You know who you are—the ones who show up and are ready for and open to the C.L.E.A.N.S.E. I am so grateful for our connection and the laughter we share. I am honored you chose to incorporate the C.L.E.A.N.S.E. into your journey.

Finally, Lord God Jesus, thank you for choosing me to channel the C.L.E.A.N.S.E. and for sending the guides who show up to give me a hand with this method.

Your emotions matter; processing them matters more.

•••

Dear Reader,

If you are intrigued by this book, it is likely you are thirsty. Not only for knowledge and insight into the topic of anxiety, but for joy. You instinctively know that having joy equals freedom from fear, worries, and insecurities. You realize that constant mind chatter is dehydrating your potential and challenging your ability to find a fluid balance in your life.

If you are feeling overwhelmed or out of control, or wish you could take a break from your constant anxiety, the process in this book can change everything. Maybe you've had a stressful upbringing, you have too much on your plate, or you find yourself awake at night worrying about your job. Whoever you are, you'll find groundbreaking insights about anxiety in these pages.

I've written and spoken about anxiety on many occasions. In 2015, the National Alliance on Mental Illness endorsed my book *The Four Gifts of Anxiety*, reinforcing my belief: Why manage anxiety when you can heal it? This led to my developing the emotional detox, a seven-step healing process that encourages you to feel your feelings without judgment, then move past them with confidence and joy. I treat the underlying causes of painful emotions in general and anxiety in particular using the seven steps contained in the acronym C.L.E.A.N.S.E.:

• <u>C</u>lear Reactivity

• <u>L</u>ook Inward

• <u>E</u>mit

- Activate Joy
- Nourish
- Surrender
- Ease

Since *Emotional Detox* was published, the method has helped thousands of people via online courses, private sessions, retreats, workshops, and trauma treatment centers. This book, *Emotional Detox for Anxiety*, is focused on anxiety, tools for building resiliency and confidence, and learning to feel your emotions rather than bury them.

Reacting to and resisting your emotions is a common practice for people with anxiety—but doing so can actually worsen your symptoms. The more you deflect your emotions, the further away a life of ease and joy will become. I totally get it—I've been there. I know what it is like to be consumed by thoughts, stuck in denial, and detached from meaningful connections. I will go as far as to say that anxiety was the way I managed the nervous energy I experienced in social situations, the pit in my stomach when I tried to speak up for myself, and the way I would jump out of bed out of fear that I would never be able to fit everything into the day ahead.

The emotional detox mindset gave me a new way to see what was happening with me and the mindful tools to set me free. I saw the symptoms of anxiety in a new light—and now you can too. Join me!

CONTENTS

PART 3: MANIFESTING JOY   193

INTRODUCTION

Anxiety and all its related thinking, analyzing, and worrying can take an immense toll on your body, mind, and spirit. You might experience aches and pains, insomnia, and indigestion...and also suffer from wear and tear on your relationships, self-esteem, productivity, stamina, creativity, and more. And you are not alone—anxiety has reached epidemic proportions, affecting more than forty million people in the United States alone. Symptoms of anxiety likely also trouble some of your coworkers, neighbors, friends, and family members—people of all ages, backgrounds, and personality types.

Until now, much of the emphasis on managing anxiety was focused on treating, preventing, and reducing the symptoms of anxiety, rather than working with emotions. Yet as I have learned in my work with people combatting anxiety, *you can't have a symptom of anxiety without an emotion.* In fact, I've found it is often the *reactions* to emotions (rather than the emotions themselves) that contribute to the symptoms of anxiety. These reactions prevent emotions from being fully processed, especially by your body.

That's where an emotional detox comes in. To address your anxiety, you need to process it through an emotional detox. Like a physical detox, an emotional detox allows you to remove unwanted impurities that prevent you from living a full and healthy life. Through an emotional detox, you can treat the underlying causes of anxiety (or any other feelings or emotions). My emotional detox process is built on a foundation of my studies of and training in many healing modalities and begins with a vivid and radical premise: *All emotions are good, even the so-called bad ones.* Just as you gain energy from food and water, when fully processed your emotions rejuvenate your parched spirit. And like with food consumption, the quality of your emotional energy is influenced by what is taken in and how it is processed. Diets laden with preservatives and chemicals are far less nutritious. Similarly, emotions overloaded with reactivity—the unsupportive ways you have learned to make the uncomfortable comfortable (like fearful thinking or denial)—clog your internal connections, making it difficult for you to be the best version of yourself.

This emotional detox journey begins with a simple choice: You can either heal or revisit what is bothering you. If you choose to heal, you will be taken on a course of exploring how to process your anxiety-related emotions instead of reacting to them. Choosing to heal and move through the seven steps of the C.L.E.A.N.S.E. is not about getting rid of your emotions. It is about getting *to* them. The process does not take long, but it is deep. Once you learn these seven C.L.E.A.N.S.E. steps and put them into practice, the method will take only a few minutes of your day. As your body begins to associate your emotions with gaining (rather than losing) energy, you will embrace what you once called anxiety and see it as an opportunity to C.L.E.A.N.S.E.

Another benefit of a C.L.E.A.N.S.E. is that it's a *lasting* way to address anxiety. You might think you have developed ways to calm your anxiety, to give yourself a break, at least for a little while. Some of these techniques might be healthy (yoga, meditation), and others (drinking, binge eating)—not so much. Regardless, the stress-releasing benefits of these efforts don't last. This is because you eventually have to address the true source of your anxiety in order to move past it—and that's what a C.L.E.A.N.S.E. will do.

A C.L.E.A.N.S.E. will give you the long-term stability and peace you have been longing for. I can't tell you how excited and grateful I am to have you on board the emotional detox journey. Take your time with the process, embrace the steps in order, and trust you are exactly where you are supposed to be right now. Allow your healing to progress naturally as you tap into your emotions as a resource for cleansing anxiety.

Let's begin…

PART 1
TOXICITY

WE ALL ENCOUNTER TOXICITY AT ONE POINT OR AN-OTHER. WE EXPERIENCE IT IN THE FORM OF CHEMICALS IN OUR FOOD AND POLLUTION IN OUR ENVIRONMENT, AND ALSO IN HOW WE REACT TO OURSELVES AND EACH OTHER. YOUR REACTIONS TO THESE TOXINS CAN HAVE AN ADVERSE EFFECT ON YOUR RELATIONSHIPS, BODIES, AND MENTAL HEALTH. YOUR CURRENT REACTIONS TO ANXIETY COULD INCLUDE LOSS OF SLEEP, TENSE MUSCLES, AND ABDOMINAL PAIN.

JUST AS YOU CAN PURIFY WATER, YOU CAN CLEANSE THESE SYMPTOMS OF ANXIETY FROM YOUR LIFE. LET'S FIRST GAIN A FULL UNDERSTANDING OF HOW THEY CAME TO BE IN YOUR LIFE IN THE FIRST PLACE.

CHAPTER 1
WHAT IS ANXIETY?

"Any decrease of anxiety is a step toward love."
—Deepak Chopra, *What Are You Hungry For?*

Before we can get into the C.L.E.A.N.S.E. and the emotional detox process it's important to understand what anxiety is, how to identify it, and where it comes from. In my work with anxiety sufferers, I've found that their most prevalent symptoms include:

- Difficulty sleeping
- Distress
- Dread
- Edginess
- Frustrations or anger
- Irritability
- Nervousness
- Self-doubt

Any of these can appear physically as:

- Excessive perspiration
- Fatigue
- Increased heart rate
- Muscle tension
- Poor memory and recall
- Stomach distress

Although it is generally agreed that there are five predominant anxiety disorders—generalized anxiety disorder, obsessive-compulsive disorder (OCD), panic disorder, post-traumatic stress disorder (PTSD), and social anxiety disorder—with myriad variations and offshoots, the common denominator is chronic worry. According to the Anxiety and Depression Association of America (ADAA), one in five people suffer from anxiety. It's such a widespread complaint that it's not unusual for individuals to self-diagnosis and, in some cases, self-medicate using various coping mechanisms. An official diagnosis might increase the likelihood that you've received medical care, but you may have found that the treatment can take you only so far, which is perhaps why you are drawn to this book.

How do you know what you're experiencing is indeed anxiety? You may hear yourself say things like:

- I am constantly on the go; I feel like I am rushing all the time.
- I am so behind in my work that I don't even know where to begin.
- I can't concentrate when my heart palpitates; I worry it is a sign I am going to have a panic attack or worse.
- I can't relax.
- I dread going somewhere new or being in a crowded room.
- I eat when I am stressed.

- I hate it when things are out of order.

- I am a procrastinator.

- I feel like people think I am a basket case.

- I feel overwhelmed and out of control.

- I find myself overreacting to the smallest things; I get so irritated and snippy.

- I have a hard time making decisions.

- I no longer feel any love or desire toward my partner.

- If only I could make more money things would be better.

- My anxiety gets worse when I am alone or not keeping busy.

- No one supports me; I feel so alone.

- No one understands how hard I am trying.

- The thought of dealing with my situation makes my heart race.

- I feel bad.

When it comes to the symptoms of anxiety, part of the C.L.E.A.N.S.E. process I'll share will be to strengthen your ability to sit confidently in these discomforts while your brain and body reshape themselves. As you'll see, the seven steps—Clear Reactivity, Look Inward, Emit, Activate Joy, Nourish, Surrender, Ease—will get you there.

Something to note: There is a difference between stress and anxiety. With stress, there is often an event or situation—a trigger—you can pinpoint, like being stuck in traffic, a work deadline, or a disagreement with a friend. Anxiety, on the other hand, can occur for no apparent reason. This means you could wake up with symptoms (and many people do) and have no idea why, which is why anxiety can make some people feel like they are losing their mind.

HOW MUCH STRESS IS TOO MUCH?

I often say stress is like salt; a little bit goes a long way. Still, we all need *some* salt and stress in our lives to function. Just like your body requires healthy levels of sodium to transmit nerve impulses and maintain a proper fluid balance, stress gives you the ability to cope and adapt to pressure and unfamiliar circumstances. Let's face it: Without a small amount of stress, you are less inclined to get out of bed, make it to work on time, fulfill your responsibilities, and take action toward fulfilling your dreams.

Your brain and body need some level of stress to learn and grow. For example, for your wrists and knees to stay healthy and strong, you have to put a little stress on your joints. The same goes for your brain: To produce new cells and neural connections, there has to be a little stress (first confusion and then problem-solving) along the way. It's the old use-it-or-lose-it mentality. In other words, you don't want a completely stress-free life, as this leads to a dull brain (and body for that matter). You are capable of so much more than that. The challenge is that if you are sensitive to any signs of discomfort in your body, it's so easy (especially in today's high-pressure world) to avoid those sensations instead of facing them. All you have to do is start thumbing through your social media or get sidetracked by all those tasks you seem to pile on your ever-growing to-do list!

On the other hand, too much stress (without awareness) can be a gateway to developing or exacerbating anxiety. If you are driving white-knuckled to your job, barking at your kids, or chugging down an energy drink due to a crappy night's sleep from too much worry, it's likely anxiety is getting the best of you. This means your brain runs for hours, ruminating on questions of *what if?* and replaying worst-case scenarios, making it difficult for you to just be. If you are feeling at the end of your rope, take it easy on yourself, as too much stress can wear on your tolerance levels. When you're under high levels of chronic stress, it can make you feel like you have more than you can handle. Proportions get skewed and even everyday activities like getting together with friends, taking a class, riding in the elevator with strangers, or walking into a well-lit room can become overwhelming.

THE ENERGY OF ANXIETY

Thanks to factors like high levels of stress and anxiety, most of us have learned to treat emotions as we would a faucet. You can turn them on, but the moment things get a little too hot or cold or uncomfortable you may be quick to turn them down or in some cases off altogether. It is exhausting to manage your emotions in this way, however. This is because your brain and body have to spend their precious time and energy on deciding whether to see something as a potential threat. Rather than relax, your brain has to be on high alert (*Is this safe to feel or not?*), which initiates a fight, flight, or freeze response.

Unfortunately, people with anxiety have gotten themselves into a lousy habit of preventing and protecting themselves from what they feel because they don't recognize the value in it. If anything, they worry that feeling too much will make their symptoms worse. So, it makes sense they would hold themselves back. Yet it is this *resistance to feeling* rather than the emotions themselves that are contributing to the symptoms of anxiety. It is kind of like putting a piece of food into your mouth but refusing to chew or swallow because you have to be preoccupied by, concentrate on, or worry about how to keep yourself from doing what is natural.

It's important to remember that your emotions don't *happen* to you, they *are* you. The sooner you embrace this fact the closer you get to joy!

Many of us have been taught to talk about our anxiety—to label and judge what is happening—which is similar to watching the trailer of a movie but never viewing the film in its entirety. You see the drama and get pulled into the action, but you never really know what happens or how the movie ends. Anxiety is similar—you get caught up in the stories, events, plots, and twists and turns. The truth of the matter is, until you take a moment to notice what is happening inside you—the energy of anxiety—you never really get the full story.

The energy of anxiety often shows up as:

- A hollow or tight sensation in the pit of your stomach
- A lump or tension in your throat and chest
- Heart palpitations or accelerated heartbeat
- Heaviness in the heart
- Nervousness, jitters, or a sense of being overwhelmed to the point where you could yell or cry
- Pressure in the head
- Stiffness or sweating in the palms of your hands
- Tightness or tension in the chest, jaw, neck, and/or shoulders

Keep in mind that anxiety's interpretation of what you're experiencing will probably be tainted by an ongoing narrative of fear. It is likely something inside you is telling you not to trust the information you are receiving. This makes life seem more unpredictable, uncertain, and untrustworthy—perhaps dangerous or threatening—which provokes more anxiety, thus creating an endless cycle.

UNDERSTANDING THE ANXIETY CYCLE

You might think that the anxiety cycle begins with an anxious or negative thought or comment, but that is not necessarily the case. The cycle starts when you hold back the inner movement of your emotions, which keeps you locked in your brain. Have you ever been around someone who says it like it is? Maybe you were thinking something negative and that person called out, "This sucks!" Perhaps that made you feel relief, like you were not alone. This relief came because calling out discomfort or a negative experience externalizes (even if only temporarily) what you may be feeling.

Since anxiety is so thought-provoking—meaning it's hard to get your mind to stop chattering—it makes sense that you might see your thoughts as the root of a problem, especially anxiety. The reality is, worrisome thoughts can happen only when your body is restricting the inner movement of energy. Since your emotions and physiological reactions to them are made of energy (molecules and atoms in motion), this means when you avoid or hold back on allowing your emotions to circulate throughout your body (e.g., constricting them to your head or shoulders or chest), you increase the likelihood of fearful or negative thoughts arising and lingering, which continues the anxiety cycle. Constricting emotions also uses up more of your mental energy. You most likely experience this as distractibility. The anxiety cycle forces energy loss and as you sense that, your symptoms likely increase. Now you're fully in the anxiety cycle *and* you have to cope with those symptoms. People with anxiety tend to use the coping skill of thinking, which leads to more energy loss (distractibility)—and the cycle goes on and on! Once you understand that emotions get processed in the body this will change.

FUEL FOR THE FIRE: COPING MECHANISMS

From what I have seen, the anxiety cycle is not only about symptoms but also includes patterns of coping—the ways in which you have learned to manage your anxiety. When you're not processing emotions, here are some ways you may be coping with the energy loss created by the anxiety cycle:

- Analyzing
- Avoiding
- Complaining
- Defending
- Drawing a blank

- Fighting
- Fixing
- Freezing, withdrawing, or clamming up
- Hiding
- Minimizing
- Overthinking
- Overpreparing
- Planning
- Pretending
- Procrastinating
- Projecting (e.g., *Why can't I stick to a healthy food plan, like her?*)
- Self-medicating

Coping mechanisms are a slippery slope. If taking another route to the grocery store and avoiding your ex-husband's house or a bridge that makes you nervous brings down your stress levels, by all means go ahead. However, if your anxiety levels are not improving, ask yourself if some of your coping mechanisms may be keeping you from processing emotions. My concern is that our over-reliance on coping has turned us into a bunch of coping addicts, spending too much energy overdosing on ways to handle the potentially next stressful thing without addressing the underlying cause, especially when it comes to anxiety. Coping only gives a temporary boost, while processing emotions (via an emotional detox) restores energy for the long term.

WHY YOU NEED TO BREAK THE ANXIETY CYCLE

Chronic anxiety is no joke. Without an intervention or treatment, it can lead to increased fatigue, muscular tension, back pain, panic attacks, breathing problems, stomachaches, migraines, depression, and more. It is not unusual to see adults (and children, for that matter) diagnosed with conditions known to be exacerbated by high levels of long-term stress. I'm talking about conditions like irritable bowel syndrome, Crohn's disease, diabetes, obesity, eating disorders, asthma, Alzheimer's, hypertension, and even addiction. In fact, many studies have shown that people with mental health disorders are at much greater risk of developing an addiction. Perhaps this is why I feel so strongly about the emotional detox method, teaching people, especially young ones, how to soothe themselves by feeling more rather than less.

DEALING WITH BRAIN WITHDRAWAL

If I were to ask you to leave your phone in the car when you went into work for the day, how would that make you feel? You might get a little nervous, preoccupied, or uncomfortable about the idea. If not your phone, then what would be the thing that would make you feel uneasy? This is what it looks and feels like when you are losing energy—you are no longer connected to the sensations that allow you to be present in your body. I call this *brain withdrawal*—the state of losing energy, possibly due to your reaction to anxiety.

In this state you are more likely to turn to quick fixes to get a burst of energy. A shot of caffeine, drugs, or even drama can be a quick fix, temporarily pushing away or masking surface discomfort. You know you are in brain withdrawal when you feel impatient and impulsive and are having a hard time being in your own skin. Put simply, brain withdrawal means you are reactive (thinking) rather than responsive (noticing, breathing).

Once, while leading a workshop on anxiety, I looked around the room and saw several people with their phones directly in front of them. When I asked one of them how they imagined it would feel if they put their phone in their bag out of reach, the participant responded, "I would feel out of control and unable to focus." In other words, her brain had become accustomed to (mis)viewing the phone as a source of energy. The challenge is, as you might have already figured out, these types of energy deposits don't last long, and they can intensify the withdrawal symptoms should they occur.

Here is the thing: Quick fixes don't work. They are good for postponing the inevitable, but ultimately they only add to the tension, causing your energy to get depleted and in some cases clogged. As this occurs, thoughts, fears, and stories increase. You imagine things as if they are really happening: *I am going to get a bad grade....My boyfriend will probably break up with me....I might not be able to get pregnant....* Get the point? You may be so good at convincing yourself that these narratives are true that you believe them. I have watched families and friendships deteriorate over things that never happened.

Here are some ways the energy-sapping state of brain withdrawal can show up and influence our lives:

- **Gossip:** You tune in to other people's business as a way to get a burst of energy. No doubt a little juicy gossip will get your adrenaline going, but these types of quick fixes can invite more conflict.

- **Negative talk:** Talking in a demeaning or harmful way about yourself or others can be a sign you are functioning on low energy; if you had adequate energy, you would be able to see more of the good.

- **Ranting:** People with anxiety tend to rant in their heads a lot, replaying conversations about what to say, what they wish would happen, and how they *really* feel about things. If this is you, it is likely you are in brain withdrawal mode.

- **Pretending:** If you are a head-nodder, telling people you are fine when you are not, then you could be in brain withdrawal. Holding on to a fantasy image of "okay" drives some people to keep going. It's a survival mechanism, but pretending everything is fine when it's not will drain your energy and eventually lead to burnout.

As your mental energy becomes dominant, your brain is likely to become really good at maintaining a beta brainwave state. Beta is usually our default waking state—alert and focused. It is the state the brain is in when we are engaged in fast, mental tasks that involve decision-making and problem-solving. When you snap your fingers and say, "Come on, let's get moving," you're in beta. It is also the state of fight, flight, or freeze, and attempting to fix a situation. The focus in beta is on getting things done on the outside rather than on processing our emotions as they're received; this can present challenges when it comes to emotions. It is not that one type of brainwave is better than another; ideally you should be oscillating throughout the day between beta (alert states) and alpha and theta (relaxation) brainwave states. Learning the C.L.E.A.N.S.E. will help you enter brainwave states that are ideal for processing emotions, and the good news is that these states are accessible. Hang in there and I will show you how.

For now, if you are in brain withdrawal there are some emotions looking to be healed and dissolved within you. Brain withdrawal can be very informative! One thing it lets you know is that whatever is disturbing you has been going on for a long time, meaning patterns and habits have formed. Resisting your emotions is partially how you have arrived at this place, yet experiencing those emotions will bring you the freedom to move through withdrawal. As when unhealthy food is not digested properly and wreaks havoc on your intestines, when your emotions are left undigested they make it difficult for you to be present, move forward, and gain the energetic nutrients your emotions are meant to provide. While you may still be hesitant to move forward, I promise you don't need to rehash, relive, or revisit the emotional charge of what happened or what was—however, you do need to honor it. One of the ways we'll begin to do that is by discovering the main sources of anxiety.

RECAP

- Anxiety is your body's way of attempting to process an emotion.

- Stress is not all bad; we need some levels of stress to function properly.

- Anxiety cycles are tricky because they include unconscious ways of coping.

- Too much focus on coping can lead to brain withdrawal.

- Withdrawal is a state of losing energy, which contributes to quick-fix strategies, most of which are unconscious.

CULTIVATE CALM

Anxiety fragments your mind, body, and spirit; your processed emotions reunite them.

CHAPTER 2
SOURCES OF ANXIETY

"The root of suffering is attachment."
—The Buddha

To honor and process anxiety, we need to understand its causes; otherwise we are more likely to resist the idea of cleansing it from our lives. A great deal of research points to genetics, environment, brain chemistry, and trauma as some of the main causes of anxiety, but in my practice I have also seen other factors, such as loneliness, financial stress, unhealthy diet/lifestyle, overuse of technology and social media, raising children, drug and alcohol addiction, and disconnection from nature, to be pretty strong contributors.

While these causes and contributors may seem too large to tackle, I have found it is our resistance to feeling that seems to be the common thread among all of these causes. If you focus on your emotions rather than on symptoms, you can influence them all. Your reactions to your emotions are what led you to your state of anxiety...and changing those reactions will move you in a new direction. Let's take a closer look at some of those causes and contributors and how emotion plays into each.

IS ANXIETY IN YOUR GENES?

Just like you can be predisposed to heart disease or addiction, your genetic makeup may contain a predisposition for anxiety. This means your DNA and how it was put together can make you more susceptible to developing symptoms of chronic worry, increased heart rate, and nervousness at some point in your life. In fact, studies like one done at the University of Wisconsin and described in *The Journal of Neuroscience* in 2018 show that when anxiety appears before age twenty, it can be an indication that a close relative passed it on to you. Before you say *thanks a lot!* to your mother or father, know that having this information can be helpful later when you C.L.E.A.N.S.E.

I'll share a piece of research that blew my mind. When scientists at the University of Wisconsin looked at the MRI brain scans of hundreds of anxious rhesus monkeys, they found significant rates of heritability. The study carefully documented monkeys from the same pedigree, noting what their neural pathways had in common. What they found was that anxious brains had similarities in the cell nuclei (the area where DNA is located) inside the part of the brain called the amygdala. While this information is critical to the future development of treatments for anxiety, what the researchers did not mention is that the amygdala is the same structure of the brain shown to play a key role in the processing of emotions.

There's more!

Research published in the journal *Neuron* in 2018 claims to have discovered brain cells in mice that seem to play a role in anxiety levels. These findings also could open the door to more effective treatments for anxiety. What I found most fascinating is these "anxiety cells" are located in the bottom of the hippocampus (the area of the brain responsible for emotional memory)! Once again, this supports how our unresolved emotions can influence our levels of anxiety.

According to Dr. Amy Przeworski of Case Western Reserve University, "Individuals inherit a predisposition to being an anxious person, [and] about 30 to 40 percent of the variability is related to genetic factors." These percentages are nothing to sneeze at. I like sharing them because anxiety often presents itself within members of the same family. Many people have the symptoms and getting to know how each of us reacts to them allows us to be more supportive and compassionate with one another.

There are certain temperament traits (inborn characteristics) that can make you more susceptible to anxiety. Some of them include:

• Sensitivity to smells, noise, and/or light

• Discomfort in crowds or crowded spaces

• Slowness to warm up or adapt to new situations

• Being highly empathic, shy, or sensitive

Once you understand how these sensitivities came to be, you are more likely to accept them (I know for me, heavily perfumed stores make me feel nauseous). As this occurs, you gradually become more tolerant.

You may be wondering what the point is of knowing whether your anxiety is partly genetic, since you can't control your DNA. Here is exciting news: You can influence (even change) your cells and your brain. Since your DNA is located in the nucleus of your cells, you can change that too! The C.L.E.A.N.S.E. works off the concept of neuroplasticity—the brain's ability to form and reorganize synaptic connections (the pathways your neurotransmitters take). Each of the seven mindful steps of the C.L.E.A.N.S.E. process includes tools proven to change the brain (e.g., visualization, meditation, and humming). While visualization and conscious breathing by themselves can change your brain, I find most people don't keep up with these kinds of practices because it may take them months to feel the benefits. I find that after just a few minutes of the C.L.E.A.N.S.E., people can feel the difference (physically, emotionally, and spiritually). When I tell them their brain had to reorganize itself to make that happen, they often feel encouraged by the process.

If any of the traits listed earlier really bother you, you can always run these beliefs and triggers through the C.L.E.A.N.S.E. (more on the how later). If you feel you have inherited anxiety, don't automatically see it in a negative light—this simply means you come from a long line of resisters. At some point, someone has got to break the chain and choose to experience and process (rather than resist) what is coming up to be healed. Because you were drawn to this book, the person most fit for this opportunity is likely to be you!

HOW YOUR BRAIN PROCESSES ANXIETY

Scientists know that there is a connection between anxiety and the limbic system of the brain, which includes structures responsible for emotional arousal, stimulation, and memory. When it comes to anxiety, researchers have observed the role two structures in the limbic system—the amygdala and the hypothalamus—play. In regard to conditions such as generalized anxiety disorder, scientists at Harvard Medical School say that the amygdala "communicates with the hypothalamus at the base of the brain, prompting quick release of hormones that raise heart rate and blood pressure, tense the muscles, and generally ready the body to fight or to flee." This means that when your brain picks up on a threat or danger, your amygdala kicks in, sending sensory information to other parts of the limbic system. This process is also what happens when your body experiences anxiety, even if there's not actually a threat to your life.

LOOKING AT STRESS THROUGH A LENS OF REACTIVITY

Some anxiety is hardwired in our brains, and some anxiety is a result of where we are and what we encounter. We now know that not all stress is bad—we need some to function—and not all symptoms of anxiety (e.g., increased heart rate, nervousness) are bad. In fact, in some cases, these symptoms represent your body's attempt to give you energy so you are prepared for the task at hand (e.g., public speaking). However, what I have found is that when suppressed emotions are present, your body has to work that much harder to generate energy. In many cases, anxiety happens not so much as a response to the task at hand, but rather because of the amount of strain you had to place on your brain and body to get through the task, including the subconscious duty of holding back your emotions. Once you begin to identify your emotions as a resource for energy rather than as something to control, this all begins to change. As a result, you are less likely to hold on to negative, fearful experiences. We will get to all that later. For now, know that anxiety can be elicited by prolonged exposure to situations that create moderate to high levels of stress.

Examples of High-Stress Situations

- Major move to a new area, job, or living situation
- Natural disasters like hurricanes or earthquakes
- Traumatic events like accidents, attacks, or injuries either experienced or witnessed
- Military service and family separation
- Loss of a job or financial instability
- Ongoing chronic health concerns either as sufferer or caregiver

Examples of Moderate-Stress Situations

- Education, homework, exams
- Social media—negative or fearful news and stories, or sense of exclusion or comparison
- Working more than one job or long hours
- Relationship difficulties
- Caring for loved ones such as small children or an elderly parent

Examples of Lower-Stress Situations

- Household tasks like paying bills or grocery shopping
- Driving in traffic
- Returning emails or texts
- Working under fluorescent lights
- Limited outdoor time or hydration

Within this context, the emotional detox journey looks at levels of anxiety differently. Rather than measuring your anxiety levels according to your symptoms (like elevated pulse or heart rate) and amount of external stress in your life (like job security), an emotional detox has a much stronger connection to how reactivity interferes with your ability to fully process your emotions.

Reactivity is defined as unsupportive ways you have learned to make the uncomfortable comfortable. It is the thoughts, beliefs, and behaviors you have both consciously and unconsciously developed as a means of resisting the digestion of your emotions. Reactivity affects people in various ways, with some experiencing higher levels than others.

High Levels of Reactivity

- You take everything personally.
- You believe you are struggling and that the people around you are not helping.
- You are your own worst critic.
- You feel exhausted and overwhelmed.
- At this level, you may quit therapy or cancel, call in sick to work, or take the risk of losing points off your final grade.

Medium Levels of Reactivity

- You are aware of your stress and symptoms.

- You know the C.L.E.A.N.S.E. can help you, but choose to carry on.

- You find some relief in coping strategies such as exercise or drinking herbal tea.

- These strategies seem to help for the short term.

Low Levels of Reactivity

- You are aware you are stressed and take a moment in your day to move through C.L.E.A.N.S.E. to process your emotions.

- You see your symptoms as an opportunity to digest some repressed emotions rather than as a setback or problem.

- You feel confident that you have a plan (e.g., C.L.E.A.N.S.E.) that can help for the long term.

In C.L.E.A.N.S.E. Step 1: Clear Reactivity, you will see how reframing your symptoms as reactivity can help. For now, let's continue looking at the causes of anxiety.

DIET AND LIFESTYLE

We all overindulge at times. (I know just one piece of cake on my birthday is not going to cut it!) When it comes to anxiety, it is not so much what you consume on any single occasion, but rather your daily diet that may or may not be contributing to your symptoms. Although individuals are unique in their physiology, many people find that certain dietary substances and habits can play a role in contributing to anxiety.

CAFFEINE

One commonly consumed substance that some people associate with anxiety is caffeine. Before you shake your head at me, this doesn't mean you have to give up your morning coffee; however, you may need to limit your intake. I know clients who have dramatically reduced their symptoms of anxiety by reducing their coffee consumption from three or four cups per day to one cup.

Here is the thing: Caffeine is known to increase your adrenaline, which elevates your heart rate. When consumed in excess (e.g., four or more cups of coffee or energy drinks per day), caffeine can leech essential vitamins and minerals (especially magnesium) from your body, making you more prone to anxiety! How do you know when you have had too much? To answer this, you have to look at the intensity of your symptoms (e.g., the quality and quantity of your sleep in relation to your caffeine intake).

SUGAR

You may want to monitor your sugar consumption a little more closely. The natural sugars found in fruit are all right, but the added sugars in most cereals, processed foods, and juices can be problematic. Anything that influences your insulin levels messes with your kidneys and liver. When these organs are overworked, your body has a difficult time relaxing. Emotions can't be processed when you are perpetually in survival mode; your internal organs need to be at ease to function properly. Certain anti-inflammatory foods, such as chamomile tea or turmeric, can support your efforts to eat less sugar.

DAIRY

To be clear: It's not the dairy itself that can cause anxiety-related problems, but rather how it is processed. Added hormones and antibiotics in cheese, milk, and butter can kill off the good bacteria in your gut, making it difficult for your body to remove toxins. Anything that interferes with your overall gut health has an impact on your brain health and the production and circulation of feel-good neurotransmitters such as serotonin. Deficiencies in serotonin can contribute to the symptoms of anxiety as well as affecting your overall mood, making it a key consideration in treating both anxiety and depression.

Some Foods That Can Increase Anxiety

• Alcohol

• Caffeinated beverages

• Dairy

• Food with lots of additives such as chemicals, dyes, or preservatives

• High-sugar or added-sugar foods

The good news is that you can give yourself a boost by consuming more of some foods, especially those containing antioxidants and certain vitamins and minerals.

Some Foods That Can Ease Anxiety

• Almonds (contain vitamin E, shown to improve mood)

• Dark chocolate (reduces the stress hormone cortisol)

• Eggs (high in vitamin D)

• Fruits (contain antioxidants)

• Pumpkin seeds (rich in potassium)

• Spinach or other vegetables high in magnesium

• Turkey (contains tryptophan, shown to improve mood)

• Turmeric, cinnamon, chamomile (anti-inflammatories)

• Wild fish like salmon (good source of omega-3 fatty acids)

BE SURE TO EAT REGULARLY

In addition to being more mindful of what you put into your mouth, don't skip meals. When you do, your blood sugar drops and you are more likely to develop panicky, worrisome thoughts. To avoid this, keep snacks such as nuts and apples handy, prepare your meals ahead, and if time is tight, consider blending a smoothie. The main thing is to not skip, because missing meals will make it difficult for you to distinguish an unprocessed emotion from hunger.

SOCIAL MEDIA

In case you have not heard, there is a new anxiety disorder in town; it's called social media anxiety disorder. Yes, this is the real deal. The Anxiety and Depression Association of America has identified how individuals experience anxiety symptoms when they are away from their social media networks for even a few minutes. If you find this hard to believe, trust me because I have seen it. I've known young women with eating disorders caught in the web of social media, spending extraordinary amounts of time thumbing through posts comparing and contrasting themselves to others. I have had clients who've lost their jobs or been involved in car accidents as a result of their incessant need to check what was happening in their social media worlds. Most of all, the people I work with talk about how much of a time-suck social media is, how they end up feeling worse after viewing it, and how they would prefer to make meaningful connections in person but don't know how to.

This current state of frayed human connection contributes to anxiety for a lot of people. The desire to find love and/or feelings of being left out are common emotions that are triggered in that online space. According to the ADAA, your social media usage has gotten out of hand if you:

- Experience physical and mental withdrawal symptoms when unable to access social media
- Keep your phone with you at all times to check your accounts
- Disengage from activities and conversations to check social media
- Lie about how much time you spend on social media

- Ignore commitments to school, work, family, or friends in favor of time on social media
- Become severely agitated when you are unable to check your notifications
- Devote more time to social media than any other activity
- Feel addicted to or unable to stay off social media accounts
- Withdraw from friends and family

Since social media is so omnipresent and has such a strong impact on our emotional and physical well-being, it is included in one of the C.L.E.A.N.S.E. samples at the end of this book. For now, ask yourself how it would feel to *not* check your social media for an hour, a day, a week. Your reaction is where some undigested emotions lie.

ISOLATION AND LONELINESS

One of the reasons we turn to social media is to alleviate loneliness, but it's not just our newsfeeds that are to blame—it was a sad day for me when I saw televisions placed in doctors' waiting rooms, grocery stores, and family restaurants. *There goes another opportunity to have a conversation with a human being.* I happen to like people; however, several of my clients with anxiety report that they don't like people. They view being social as a drag or fake. Perhaps this view is due to the onslaught of social media and the negative political climate. However, when I probe my clients on this, they often admit that they don't feel like they can be themselves with others.

It is common for people with anxiety to avoid social situations. These situations can often trigger symptoms such as increased heart rate, feelings of being overwhelmed, and nervousness. Rather than deal with the discomfort and fear that the symptoms will get worse (e.g., panic), someone with anxiety might choose to forgo the situation altogether. This leads to a cycle that is challenging to overcome:

When people continually avoid social situations, their feelings of awkwardness and discomfort only increase as they never have the opportunity to learn to comfortably negotiate such experiences. Perhaps this is why people with anxiety can seem like they have limited social skills. For example, they might avoid eye contact, mix up their words, bite their nails, or exhibit nervous laughter.

This social awkwardness can lead to loneliness. People need human interaction, connection, love, and support to thrive. If you tend to limit your relationships, communicate mainly via text or video games, or spend large amounts of time alone, consider moving some of your fears and anxieties through the C.L.E.A.N.S.E. You will learn how to do this in Part 2, where the C.L.E.A.N.S.E. steps are described in detail. Keep in mind you do not have the formula yet, so please avoid jumping ahead. This will all make sense soon, I promise.

RECAP

- Social media, diet, and disconnection are significant contributors to anxiety.
- Understanding the roots of anxiety helps you understand the triggers.
- You can help clear the causes of anxiety by placing them into the C.L.E.A.N.S.E.
- Reframing "symptoms" as "reactivity" sets the tone for a C.L.E.A.N.S.E.

CULTIVATE CALM

Sometimes the bravest thing you can do is to simply feel your emotions.

CHAPTER 3
WHAT IS AN EMOTIONAL DETOX?

*"They may forget what you said,
but they will never forget how you made them feel."*
—Carl W. Buehner

Now that you have some background on chronic anxiety and the negative effects it can have on your body and mind, let's talk about how you can get rid of that burden using an emotional detox. Like a physical detox, an emotional detox removes unwanted impurities (in this case, your reactions to anxiety) that prevent you from living a full and healthy life. In essence, an emotional detox is a systematic and mindful way to purge undigested emotions stuck inside you. Completing an emotional detox will allow you to truly feel your emotions, teach you how to take care of your feelings, and provide a road map for living a happy, fulfilled life.

DETOXING HELPS YOU LEARN TO FEEL YOUR EMOTIONS

One key point about an emotional detox: You will not be getting rid of your emotions. Sorry, that is not the plan. Instead, you change your reactions to emotions. It bears repeating: It's your reactions—the ways in which you have learned to reject, ignore, and resist the flow of your emotions—not the emotions themselves that are contributing to your anxiety.

While some people may think feeling your emotions is not a big deal, I assure you that for someone with anxiety it is a big deal! I have found that people with anxiety are *terrified* of their emotions. They have dedicated an enormous amount of time, energy, willpower, and even money to controlling or escaping them. As a result, they have developed the self-sabotaging unconscious coping mechanisms we looked at earlier, such as fleeing, freezing, drawing a blank, crying, breaking down, and more. This is because anxiety—which most of us think of as a feeling—is actually a reaction to non-feeling, and the symptoms you experience (like ruminating, panic, withdrawing, and more) are ways you have coped with anxiety.

It is time to turn this ship around and recognize how the symptoms of anxiety that you experience may be a form of coping with non-feeling in disguise. You see, these reactions suck up a lot of energy, and the more you recognize them for what they are, the less likely you will be to fuel them. Instead you will say to yourself: *Okay, I am in reactivity and I am going to feel (rather than rehearse via thinking) what is coming up.*

Marlin had a habit of letting people around her know she was stressed and anxious. As a result, they would give her unsolicited advice. Go exercise, you will feel better…drink water…breathe…don't worry so much. Hearing this advice only made Marlin worse. She felt so much pressure and now she had to figure out a way to exercise, drink more, etc. Ugh! As a result, she coped with this added pressure by crying, getting mad, breaking down, and avoiding further conversations. It wasn't until Marlin took up the C.L.E.A.N.S.E. method and learned the difference between coping and feeling that she experienced her emotions instead of diverting them, which changed her for the better.

To someone with anxiety, the mere thought of allowing emotions to be experienced can be gut wrenching. My work with clients has taught me that people with anxiety often have a subconscious belief that feeling their emotions somehow makes them powerless. This couldn't be further from the truth. This is what makes C.L.E.A.N.S.E. a revolutionary method for emotions in general and anxiety in particular—you will reclaim that power.

Right now, you may be thinking, *I feel my feelings. I am constantly worried, upset, or rattled.* However, as you will learn on this journey to C.L.E.A.N.S.E. anxiety, the act of worrying is not feeling, it is reacting. I am pleased to tell you: Feeling does not equal pain; holding back your emotions is what causes pain. This means if worrying, dread, and stress are keeping you up at night, or encouraging you to distance yourself from others or reach for quick fixes such as drugs or alcohol, you are not feeling much at all.

WELCOMING THE UNKNOWN

What do you imagine the detox process will be like? What are some of the stories you have been telling yourself about anxiety, your emotions, and the unknown? Do you believe processing your emotions will be painful, long, and stressful? Are you convinced you already have more than you can handle?

If you think your emotions are something to avoid, then it makes sense you might avoid digesting them raw and whole. If you have doused them in salt to hide the real flavor, to stay "strong" and to keep the status quo, slow down and take a moment to savor your emotions in their pure form. Perhaps you have chosen to alter (or in some cases numb) sensations in another way like drinking or binge-watching Netflix. I totally get it; I once had my tricks for shutting down and turning my head away from what was bothering me. I didn't know it at the time, but I was shutting down joy.

As you start this journey away from anxiety, associated stress, brain withdrawal, and attaching to coping, you may have no idea where you will end up—and that is exactly how it is supposed to be. You've been using these tools for a long time (even though they were not "fixing" anything), and undoing those habits can be scary at first! I want you to assume the unknown is exactly what you need right now. Think of it as an essential vitamin you have been low on. This may be challenging if you are used to being in control, even (and especially) if your life feels unmanageable. I know it was for me during my own emotional detox. To support the detox, treat the unknown as an asset, a natural remedy to set you free from all the worry and angst—both indicators of anxiety.

WHY YOU COULD USE A DETOX (ESPECIALLY IF YOU'RE ANXIOUS)

Perhaps there is a part of you that is not sure this journey is right for you. Maybe because deep down inside, you are still waiting for others to deal with *their* issues. This is because right now you are approaching emotions from old mindsets and patterns. Once you discover how empowering this process is, you will free these patterns and look forward to having a relationship (rather than a conflict) with your emotions. What matters is that you allow yourself to *feel* again. Emotions that are pushed away are left undigested in your body. While this way of seeing, of describing what is happening to you right now, may seem unfamiliar, using this new emotional detox terminology will help you reshape your perspective.

Everyone in your world will benefit from you stepping into this. While that might not be enticing to someone who has cut off their relationship with their father or who wants nothing to do with their ex, know that holding on to old resentments will hurt you far more than it will hurt them. While you might believe your resistance somehow illustrates your disapproval for what they did or did not do, it's likely you are the one who is most malnourished from this way of reacting; hence the thirst.

You might not be able to see it right now, but this process strengthens you. I have watched people terrified of speaking up suddenly find their voice again. In addition to the symptoms of anxiety discussed in Chapter 1, if any of the following characteristics apply to you, an emotional detox could help you access your authentic emotions.

Signs You Could Benefit from an Emotional Detox

- You overempathize with others, meaning you give them excuses for their poor behavior.

- You are attached to details or making things better.

- You often feel overextended, rushed, and overwhelmed.*

- You strive for perfection and put a lot of pressure on yourself to do everything right.*

- You tend to want to fix rather than feel what is happening.

- You overfocus on others, leaving little to no time for yourself.*

- You often feel guilty or bad.

- You judge yourself or others.

- You freeze easily or draw a blank when you feel pressured.*

- You are quick to want to fix or make discomfort go away.*

- You are easily insulted or take things personally.

- You shut down or withdraw from others when things get uncomfortable.

- You are afraid of the past and prefer not to talk about the future.

- You were raised to believe feelings were bad or weak and expressing them would burden others.

- You don't know how to feel your emotions; you believe you have to talk about them.

- You were betrayed or blindsided by someone at some point in your life.

*Signs specific to anxiety.

Some other signs that you might be ready for an emotional detox include:

- You drink or take drugs to escape the pressures in life.

- You are easily swayed by the opinions of others.

- You overeat (or undereat) when you are upset.

- You feel like you work hard but nothing changes.

- You are financially insecure.

- You have been losing or gaining weight.

- You experience self-doubt and second-guessing.

- You have trouble speaking up for yourself.

- You feel uncomfortable listening to other people talk about their feelings.

THE PURPOSE OF AN EMOTIONAL DETOX

The purpose of an emotional detox is to allow you to discover the tremendous value of your emotions. An emotional detox is an opportunity, not an outcome. Your attachment to outcome (e.g., wanting things to be better, easier, more manageable) may well be a reaction to undigested emotions that are showing up as anxiety. This book will help you dismantle the walls you have so diligently constructed around your emotions. While at one point these walls may have served you, that is no longer the case if you are experiencing symptoms of anxiety.

Again, the point of a detox is *not* to stop having feelings or reactions altogether. When you deny your feelings through avoidance behaviors (such as overfocusing on others or dulling feelings), you diminish the healing power your emotions have to offer. By doing so, you never get to know what it would feel like to live to your fullest potential.

WHAT YOU WILL LEARN

One of the most significant things you will learn in this emotional detox process is that everything has purpose, even anxiety! I would even go out on a limb and say that what you will learn is that your emotions are connected to your personal sense of purpose and that feeling your emotions contributes to your well-being and benefits our world at large.

Nothing has taught me more than being a student and teacher of the C.L.E.A.N.S.E. method. This is because when you allow yourself to fully digest your emotions, the information you receive is pure, meaning direct from your source. To me, feeling my emotions is no different than experiencing God. In many ways, I see myself in service, taking a personal vow to pass on this information as clearly as I can so that you too can experience the small miracles I have seen. People with significant wounds and trauma can become stronger, more confident, understanding, and compassionate toward themselves and others.

You'll also learn:

- What your emotions are, and what they are not
- The way reactivity shows up in your life

- How to digest rather than react to (e.g., think or worry about) an emotion
- How to communicate from nondefensiveness
- What happens in your body when you are triggered
- What the symptoms of anxiety are really attempting to tell you
- Ways you block the flow of your emotions as well as ways to enhance their flow
- How to listen to (rather than react to) your bodily feedback
- A seven-step C.L.E.A.N.S.E. plan for addressing the symptoms of anxiety

And so much more…

THINGS TO AVOID DURING YOUR DETOX

Like a plant-based diet or a regular exercise routine, an emotional detox is a lifestyle. People starting a diet have made a conscious decision to avoid or decrease their consumption of certain foods. Similarly, those who choose the pathway of an emotional detox have made a conscious decision to digest (process) emotions, heal, and not consume reactivity. Most people I know who choose this lifestyle are clear that it is a personal choice and are mindful not to judge others. You may choose to digest, while others may continue to consume reactivity. That is their choice, and to truly be on a detox journey we must respect each other's ways.

An emotional detox is similar to a diet in that people often lapse and binge on chocolate, for example. Overconsumption is also a common strategy that people use to avoid emotions. It's important to be aware of things you may be overconsuming to avoid emotions. The following are common emotion-avoiding "crutches" that you should try to avoid during your detox:

- Alcohol or other mood-altering substances
- Excessive caffeine intake
- Carbonated beverages (they interrupt digestion)
- Eating late at night (this can interrupt sleep)
- Nonprescription medication
- Social media and Internet surfing
- Sugary and high-sodium foods or beverages
- Obsessively watching the news

The bottom line is that you want to be mindful of anything that causes you inflammation, both physically and mentally. This is because you want the information pathway between your brain and your body to be clear, and inflammation causes confusion along this route. As a psychology professor, I am always teaching, learning, and talking about the brain. When it comes to anxiety, your brain has been wired to operate a certain way, yet your emotions (when in flow) can change the course of that process.

GOING RAW

Think about a fresh apple from the farmers' market versus a piece of apple-flavored candy that's been processed, sometimes with chemicals, and loaded up with sugar. The apple candy is far less nutritious and could even harm your system. The fresh apple will taste better, be easier to digest, and nourish you in a way a piece of apple-flavored candy can't.

It's the same with emotions. "Going raw" means digesting your pure emotions as they are, unfiltered by your fears and anxieties. When your emotions have been marinated in reactivity, you are more likely to resort to behaviors that overprocess them, such as thinking, analyzing, defending, and minimizing your strengths and abilities.

Processing your emotions widens your lens, giving you the full scope of your attributes and possibilities, but overprocessing leaves you bombarded, frustrated, and hopeless.

The main difference you will see between going raw and overprocessing is choice. When you go raw, it means you are choosing to digest an emotion *as is* without revisiting all that reactivity. When you overprocess, it is likely you are running on autopilot (kind of like those fearful, worried thoughts). With that said, similar to how it would be if you chose to go vegan, going raw takes some awareness, some knowledge, and a certain amount of skill, with a little guidance along the way always coming in handy.

The rawer you get, the more energy you gain. Energy is essential to creating the life you want—one of deeper, more meaningful relationships, acceptance, and love. To let go of old ways and open to new possibilities, you need energetic fuel; without it, you are likely to stay consumed, stuck, or hung up in old patterns. The good news is that no trips to the market or pharmacy are necessary—a shift in awareness is all it takes.

The following table lists some of the factors that support overprocessed emotions and depleted energy, and shows the increased-energy factors they can be transformed into by going raw with your emotions:

INCREASE ENERGY	DEPLETE ENERGY
Feeling	Thinking
Noticing	Projecting
Observing	Reacting
Compassion	Criticism
Focusing	Distraction
Allowing	Analyzing

Let's consider how this plays out. Perhaps you feel a tightness in your chest in anticipation of taking on extra hours at work. As your heart rate increases (a sign of anxiety), you become more tense. In response to the tension and elevated heart rate, you tell one of your kids or your roommate to be quiet, to settle down (reaction). You start thinking about how much is on your plate (reaction). You ruminate about how disrespectful your kid or roommate is (reaction). This makes things feel more intense and as a result you experience an increase of nervousness and pressure (anxiety).

Using this example, the difference between overprocessing and going raw would be to notice the tension in your chest and feel the urge to scold someone but then *choose to process* the emotions that are surfacing along with the reactions. When you choose to process your feelings, you give yourself real, authentic, raw energy instead of feeding your anxiety. During these moments, going outside for a breath of fresh air will help. When you learn to combine Step 1 of the C.L.E.A.N.S.E. method (Clear Reactivity) with taking a breath, that is when you know you are truly choosing to process instead of react.

HEALING VERSUS RECOVERING

Your detox journey is about generating a healing inner space so that emotions become a form of nourishment, freedom, motivation, and guidance. You may not know which emotions you need to work on right now or whether they are worth the effort; however, I want you to trust that you are worth it! Know that an emotional detox will never hurt you, but living with anxiety can. You can only gain from this experience, and anything that helps you will inevitably have a positive influence on others.

Emotional detoxes are opportunities, not detours. They help you find the best path, and not overcomplicate things. They are about healing, not recovering. This is not to say there isn't a place or time for that; however, during an emotional detox, seeing yourself "in recovery" may be a way to hold yourself back from opening to the possibilities, leading you to manage your emotions instead of *experiencing* them. This is because recovery has many interpretations—sometimes it can mean there is a chance for a relapse while other times it means heading toward a cure. Healing, on the other hand, is about returning to wholeness. This is more in line with the detox mindset. It is important you understand that C.L.E.A.N.S.E. is by no means about "fixing" yourself. You are already good enough!

People may overprocess their emotions because they see this as a way to support their recovery. For example, I once had a client in recovery who was struggling with a couple of coworkers. She mentioned to me that in her recovery program she had been taught to "keep your mouth shut and mind your own business." While this type of thinking can help you get through some situations, I have found in working with people who previously managed their anxiety via addiction that when they tell themselves to keep their mouths shut, this can (without awareness) push down their emotions. I am not saying there are never times when living by this motto might be helpful; however, if it is causing you to react (hold back) your emotions you are depriving yourself from the energy of your raw emotions, an energy that has the capacity to heal your anxiety.

It happens—if you associate a feeling with an old insult or emotional wound or relapse, then how you have been handling your anxiety makes perfect sense. Notice how you might beat yourself up if you eat a piece of cake after you have vowed to lay off the sweets or if you take on an overwhelming task as your life is becoming more balanced. Rather than get yourself all in a tizzy, give yourself a moment to pause.

Recovery mindsets have a way of making us doubt our abilities and believe that whatever it is we are trying to avoid, stop, or change is going to happen again. This happens more often than you may think. Drive in busy traffic, spend some time talking to your mother about her problems, or work an extra-long day, and you will see the shift. This is because we get hooked into a larger consciousness—a collection of people who feel the same way (overextended, rushed, disconnected)—and before we know it, we are all intoxicated with anxiety. If you are fully embracing your healing and have no fear about a setback or relapse, a recovery mindset may not interrupt the detox. However, if there is an ounce of doubt, it may.

Your emotions don't fix you; they *are* you. When you truly get this, you will become your whole self. That's why the C.L.E.A.N.S.E. method is such an effective and authentic way to work with, understand, and alleviate anxiety.

STAYING ON COURSE

Once you learn about your emotions—how they tie into anxiety and how avoiding processing them fuels your symptoms—you will make subtle (and not-so-subtle) changes in how you react to day-to-day experiences. You will learn how strong emotions may be re-exposing you to trauma when you dwell on the past and allow your imagination to run wild. The C.L.E.A.N.S.E. will show you how to process the emotions that are underdeveloped or stifled within your brain and body before things spin out of control and you find yourself impatient, agitated, burning the midnight oil, stressing out, lashing back with a slew of text messages, or experiencing a full-blown anxiety attack.

This will take faith, which brings us back to embracing the unknown. I am not exaggerating when I say that this process will bring you closer to your higher power. Doubt is a reaction, not an emotion, and I believe that anxiety is a reaction as well. Should doubt and anxiety occur (and they will!), pause, take a deep breath, and invite them in, because behind all that reactivity is an opportunity to return to wholeness. While that may not make sense to you right now, trust that once you move through the C.L.E.A.N.S.E. steps it will!

RECAP

- An emotional detox is a mindful, seven-step process for learning how to feel your emotions.

- Anxiety is a reaction, and in the emotional detox journey we clear reactions, not emotions.

- Avoiding or ignoring your emotions may re-expose you to previous traumas and wounds.

- Emotional detox is a way to gain insight, learn, and grow from your past experiences and reactions.

CULTIVATE CALM

Anxiety taught you what happens when you don't feel. Give thanks for what was and for knowing that you now have the wherewithal to choose differently.

CHAPTER 4

THE BENEFITS OF AN ANXIETY DETOX

"What makes you vulnerable makes you beautiful."
—Brené Brown

As you release old habits of reactivity, your emotions are permitted to circulate more freely, and as a result your entire bodily system will experience benefits. When I practice C.L.E.A.N.S.E., I have increased physical stamina and mental strength. This is because circulated emotions provide a cleaner energy that better supplies your body with what it needs to operate on all cylinders. As you'll see in this chapter, when unblocked by reactivity, your emotions have the capacity to reduce inflammation, shift judgmental patterns, relinquish fear, nurture resiliency and connection, and supercharge your manifesting abilities—all of which will ease—and many times eliminate—anxiety.

Even how you take a rest will change. Rather than collapsing from mental or physical exhaustion, complaining about how few breaks you get, or giving yourself a temporary hit of reactivity by engaging in social drama, you will notice the early indications of anxiety and give yourself the opportunity to heal from them. Once you experience the benefits of processing your emotions, you will be less likely to push yourself to the edge or burn out those adrenal glands with worrisome thinking. This is because as you raise your energy, your awareness level increases, and you will have a new outlook on life. There is something really refreshing about living in a state of nonattachment. It gives you a sense of calmness like nothing else, and the moment will come when you suddenly realize the universe really is working in your favor.

REDUCING INFLAMMATION

It's been well established by doctors and researchers that prolonged high levels of stress contribute to bodily inflammation. According to research from Pennsylvania State University, sorrow, rage, and other negative emotions can actually create inflammation in your body, which makes you more prone to pain and pain-related ailments like rheumatoid arthritis.

I've seen this with my clients. It is common for them to speak about weight gain, chronic tension, back pain, and sciatic or gastrointestinal problems due to years of living with anxiety. This is because, similar to how saturated fats clog your arteries, suppressed emotions clog up your meridian system (the invisible energy pathways or channels that run through your body and circulate your life-force energy). As you feel rather than react to your emotions, your blood flow will increase, providing a natural, anti-inflammatory response in your body.

Here is the thing: Withheld and trapped emotions grip your energy (as well as your organs), causing you to feel on edge. This increases the likelihood that you will develop self-sabotaging attitudes and behaviors such as hiding (lying) or ignoring (pretending). The emotional detox journey relieves this pressure, providing you a means for releasing those muscles, glands, and organs. As you liberate the fight, flight, or freeze response, your organs no longer have to restrain your emotional flow, and as this occurs, your body begins to function opti-mally with the absence of inflammation.

I once worked with a client who could not find a job. After a few minutes of listening to her, it was clear it wasn't because she wasn't qualified. In fact, her resume was quite impressive. What I did notice was that she told me a long-winded story about a past car accident, the aches and pains it left her as she underwent months of physical therapy, along with bouts of post-traumatic stress disorder. The trauma of not just the accident but the months of recovery (leaving her out of work) created more space for reactivity, intensifying her anxiety. It wasn't until she gave herself a chance to digest the incident fully (without re-running the trauma through her brain) that things began to move in a more positive direction.

Neuroscientist Candace B. Pert, author of *Molecules of Emotion: The Science Behind Mind-Body Medicine*, began looking at the connections between emotions and inflammation back in 1984. She introduced evidence showing how various parts of our bodies communicate via chemical messengers—neuropeptides and their receptors. For exam-ple, the brain sends signals to the gallbladder, and the stomach sends signals to the brain. Neurons from the brain communicate with your stomach to initiate digestion. However, if your body is in the flight, flight, or freeze response, your brain and body will believe it is in a state of emergency and therefore digestion will be put off. In order to have a healthy flow of emotions, you need internal movement, including your body's ability to relax so you can excrete waste. Your internal state (energy movement) impacts the way you see the world and thus your belief system. As you learn the C.L.E.A.N.S.E., the dia-logue between your mind and body will make more sense. Rather than getting sidetracked by the symptoms of anxiety, you will be able to soothe inflamed thoughts by tapping into the incredible communica-tion network tied in with your emotions.

MANAGING WEIGHT AND ENERGY LEVELS

After I taught a C.L.E.A.N.S.E. yoga class, a student asked me, "Will this class help me get rid of that last ten pounds?" I smiled and replied, "Along with whole foods and exercise, yes, it will."

Here's how a C.L.E.A.N.S.E. can help you manage weight. When you are under chronic stress, your body secretes the hormone cortisol, which is known to increase insulin production. Excess insulin production can cause cravings for sweet and high-fat foods. An emotional detox (along with a balanced healthy lifestyle that includes regular exercise and good nutrition) can help because you will experience chronic stress far less often and thus some of those cravings might decrease.

Regular exercise can help you manage anxiety and weight—but only in the short term. According to the Anxiety and Depression Association of America, many of the benefits of exercise are temporary. The ADAA acknowledges that "science has also provided some evidence that physically active people have lower rates of anxiety and depression than sedentary people" but goes on to say, "Although the effects may be temporary, they demonstrate that a brisk walk or other simple activity can deliver several hours of relief, similar to taking an aspirin for a headache." I have found that when you blend the mindset of an emotional detox with physical exercise, the energy you receive is long-lasting.

SHIFTING JUDGMENTAL PATTERNS

The energy from processed emotions elevates you to a level of understanding that can be difficult to obtain when you are resisting your emotions. Through this elevated awareness, you will be able to view yourself and others in a different light. You will be less likely to judge yourself and others, because you will recognize and acknowledge the emotions that reside within this unconscious habit.

WHAT DOES JUDGMENT LOOK AND SOUND LIKE?

Judgment often shows up in the form of thinking. Thoughts such as *that person is so rude* or *she is clueless* are a form of judgment. It can also show up as self-criticism such as *I am so fat* or *I am such a space shot*. What I have found is that judgment is often the glue that holds reactive patterns together. With that said, you are human and if you are having a judgmental thought, I suggest you embrace it and run it through the C.L.E.A.N.S.E.; otherwise you are going to have to exert a tremendous amount of energy pretending that the thought doesn't exist.

Judgment is one of the ways you may have learned to cope with anxiety. If you judge something by calling it a name, that is another way to try to control it. For example, you might label someone as a bad parent or an impatient teacher. While they may certainly have room for improvement, consider that this label may be a way you are managing your anxiety around the situation. When you no longer feel the need to judge yourself or others, you will have changed that pattern and therefore won't need that coping mechanism.

When I run judgment through the C.L.E.A.N.S.E., I often find that it was being propelled by feelings of fear and insecurity. If these buried emotions are not allowed to move, they can lead to condescending and at times manipulative behaviors. That's likely what has happened when you see a person who claims they are for the rights of women suddenly caught in a sexual harassment scandal. While on the outside this person might look like a creep, fake, or traitor, on the inside they found a rather intense way to manage (act out) emotions of fear and rage. By no means does this excuse their behavior nor should they be spared the consequences; however, it does illustrate how deeply entrenched patterns can be. The roots can run so deep that the person's outward-facing persona seems totally disconnected from the inner emotions that are motivating their behavior.

BREATHING EXERCISE TO CONNECT TO YOUR EMOTIONS WITHOUT JUDGMENT

One way to experience your emotions without judgment is to become aware of your breathing. Some situations or circumstances (especially those that are rooted in anxiety, stress, fear, or judgment) cause you to hold your breath or become breathless. In these moments, you are in a state of minimal feeling or non-feeling. The pattern lies within the fabric of your breath. Becoming aware of your breathing and learning to observe without reliving (judging) the past is the route to inner freedom. So that you can experience this yourself, take a moment now and breathe.

1. Sit up tall with your two feet on the floor.

2. Observe your breath.

3. Settle into your body by rolling your neck and shoulders around.

4. Notice how your breathing shifts to either an inhale or an exhale.

When you choose to experience rather than judge your emotions, you are contributing to ending old cycles of fear and anxiety.

LETTING GO OF FEAR

If you have a long history of anxiety, you may see yourself as broken. This is because you have become accustomed to viewing your emotions as a sign that there is a problem. Before practicing the C.L.E.A.N.S.E., I viewed myself that way as well. Although I didn't have conscious thoughts of being broken, my actions leaned that way. As a result, I tried all sorts of therapy and energy healing. While these experiences were informative, looking back I realize it was how they got me connected to other people that really jump-started change.

It wasn't until I started practicing the C.L.E.A.N.S.E. method that I began to see a shift from fear to curiosity. *I bet you thought I was gonna say love, right?* What I learned is that curiosity is a precursor to love. As I assisted hundreds of students and clients through the C.L.E.A.N.S.E., they too reported feeling more curious, interested, open, and willing. These are all signs that patterns are completing, and fear is releasing.

Since the pop psychology and media industries are typically on the side of non-feeling, you have to really commit yourself to this process. Stay strong, and no matter what is happening (like fearful news), stand in the power of your emotions. Refrain from trusting others who claim they are going to banish your fear or anxiety with one quick fix—these promises come in many forms. You can see it in marketing, such as a message that says if you visit a resort or sign up for an online workshop everything will be okay. While we could all benefit from a nice relaxing vacation or some great therapy, the reality is that *only you have the power to feel your own emotions.* No one else and no great locale can do it for you. The good news is that you don't need money to do it.

Anxiety is how you are coping with *not* feeling, so when you resort to fearful measures or quick-fix remedies, you are putting off the benefits that can be available to you at any time. When you come to understand this your fear will transform into love.

FEAR	LOVE
Escapes	Connects
Freezes	Dissolves
Closes	Opens
Fights off	Reconciles
Wounds	Mends

See the differences between the two states? Moving toward love will have an amazing impact on your life.

NURTURING RESILIENCE INSTEAD OF SYMPATHY

After years of working with people with anxiety, one of the common traits I have found is that people with anxiety tend to be highly empathic. This means they are quick to pick up on the energy of others. For example, you might feel so bad for someone that you spend all your free time helping them and forget even basic self-care such as drinking an adequate amount of water or going out for some fresh air to nurture yourself. Without the skills to handle this attribute, you can intensify the symptoms of anxiety. Moving through the C.L.E.A.N.S.E. method on a regular basis will build up your emotional immune system, allowing you to be less susceptible to picking up the lower vibrations (sadness, fear, anger) in others. This allows you to be more compassionate rather than sympathetic to their situation. The energy of compassion sustains you, while sympathy without awareness can be draining.

Before you get too hard on yourself for overstepping your boundaries, listen, I totally get it; I too have had my fair share of being walloped by being an empath. I remember plenty of days when I had to take a two-hour nap after working with a client! The gift and challenge of sensing energy in others without awareness is that you can tune in so deeply that you believe it is *your* energy. For example, you might sit next to someone who is struggling with depression and suddenly start to have negative or sad thoughts about yourself. Ask yourself if this is truly the way you feel or if you have picked up someone else's emotions.

The truth of the matter is that anxiety is contagious. You can feel it and sense it when it is around you. If this section rings true, I assure you that moving through an emotional detox will bring you great relief. Keep being yourself and keep your heart open—however, know when it is time to back off, and trust that the more resilient you are, the more you will be connected with others and the earth in a meaningful way.

Think of it this way: People can pick up on your anxiety, right? Well, they can also sense your strength; and when they do, that is when you can become a force for good. The more you experience your emotions, the less need you will have to protect yourself. Instead, you will find comfort, safety, and strength in the flow of your emotions.

SUPERCHARGING MANIFESTING!

I would be remiss if I didn't mention how an emotional detox supercharges your manifesting potential. When I say "manifesting," I mean bringing something forth in your physical life through the process of digesting your emotions. By now you know your emotions give you energy, right? Well, when you take that newfound energy and aim it toward what you are choosing to create—in this case peace, calm, and happiness—you are in fact manifesting. Whether you realize it or not, you are always co-creating something. The challenge comes when you are accidentally co-creating something you don't want, like having to cope with symptoms of anxiety.

The coolest part about manifesting through an emotional detox is that it happens without effort. Clients who began working with me to get rid of their symptoms of anxiety would suddenly share how a job offer came their way, they got a promotion at work, they became pregnant, or a relationship that was once adversarial was beginning to mend. One client even found relief from debt!

Amy had been out of work for some time. In fact, she even hesitated to come see me about her anxiety because her finances were so tight, making her even more anxious. After a few sessions she told me she went to the gym and started chatting with the woman next to her on the elliptical machine. It turned out the woman knew a ton of people in Amy's industry and suggested Amy send her resume and she would forward it to some of her contacts. Amy told me how normally at the gym she tried to avoid eye contact and keep to herself; however, her newfound energy from processing her emotions opened her up and she gave off a vibe of friendliness. Eventually she was able to move forward with one of the contacts and land a job, which led to her paying off her debt!

When you don't allow yourself to feel, you are more likely to close down rather than open up to new opportunities; people will respond to this, even if it's subconsciously. As you learn to manifest with your emotions, people will be drawn to you. Connections are made and things fall into place. Just as the energy of your emotions is infinite, so is your ability to manifest. I am so excited you are on this journey!

RECAP

The benefits of an emotional detox are:

- Your physical, mental, and spiritual energy increases.
- You become less judgmental of yourself and others.
- You are less apt to pick up on the negativity or anxiety in others.
- You learn how to care for yourself.
- You create what you want, rather than what you don't want.
- The more energy you gain, the more relaxed and connected you become.

CULTIVATE CALM

Anxiety is a pattern of energy; thoughts don't alter patterns, feelings do!

CHAPTER 5

WHAT ARE WE DETOXING WHEN WE CLEANSE ANXIETY?

"The beginning of anxiety is the end of faith,
and the beginning of true faith is the end of anxiety."
—George Müller

While it may seem like your emotions—feeling worried, nervous, and fearful—are causing you to experience anxiety, what you will be detoxing is your reactions, not your emotions. This is because it is your reactions that are keeping you trapped in the anxiety loop. To help you break this cycle, I have found that reframing symptoms as reactivity makes a huge difference.

As I've said before, reactivity is defined as unsupportive ways you have learned to make the uncomfortable comfortable. It is thoughts, beliefs, and behaviors you have consciously and unconsciously developed as a means of resisting the digestion of your emotions. As this occurs, your emotions become overprocessed; and like overprocessed food, this is not healthy. But instead of being laden with chemicals and preservatives, your emotions become contaminated by reactivity (things like paranoia, worry, and panic). Resistance causes reactivity! Detoxing your anxiety means you will be detoxing all the ways you have been resisting your emotions, things like internalizing, externalizing, perfectionism, narrating, and attaching to coping. Let's start this conversation by taking a closer look at resistance.

RESISTING YOUR EMOTIONS

Resistance happens when you attempt to keep yourself from experiencing an emotion. Before you get too hard on yourself, know that most of us have been taught to refrain from feeling our emotions. If you were raised in the sit-down-and-keep-your-mouth-shut era you know what I am talking about. Some of the younger generations have had similar influences, although the delivery has been different. Technology has had a big impact; when communication is accomplished mainly digitally, the act of feeling emotions may be lost in translation. The increased use of technology to receive and send information sometimes leads to emotional nuances being overlooked. Even our doctors' offices tell us to download apps to get our own medical information. Gone are the days of face-to-face interactions and with that comes some emotional suppression. While this is all intended to make life easier, I am not sure if your life can truly feel easier without emotional flow. While it can be fun and quick to text an emoji or send a Snap, it really doesn't do anything on the level of your emotional energy. This is why I am a big advocate for the C.L.E.A.N.S.E.; this process helps you to access and feel your authentic emotions. What you resist persists and, in this case, it is the signs, symptoms, and intensity of your anxiety that will hinder your growth.

I have found that the two predominant ways that people resist emotions are through repression and suppression. Let's learn more about each.

SUPPRESSION

When you suppress an emotion, you are making a conscious decision not to let it move. You are aware of the discomfort, bothersome thoughts, and fears, but you make an active choice to bury the emotion and pretend you are fine. In some cases, repression can be healthy. For example, if there is a party and you have to study for an exam, you might consciously choose not to think about or allow your feelings about the party to come up. This presents a challenge though, because the thoughts and feelings are not likely to disappear and might show up in another way. From the emotional detox perspective, you are way better off taking a moment to C.L.E.A.N.S.E. than spending your precious time and energy constantly redirecting yourself back to task.

Avoiding conflict is another way you may suppress your emotions. For example, you may know someone is upset, which makes you feel uncomfortable, tense, and nervous. Rather than experience your emotions, you decide to avoid that person. The problem is that these kinds of approaches can wither self-esteem and prevent you from accessing the healing power of your emotions, while weakening your ability to communicate and connect with others. If someone is potentially destructive or dangerous to be around, by all means, stay clear. However, if it is someone who is upset or perhaps overwhelmed or hurt, pause and digest what is coming up inside *you*. This will be far more helpful than trying to figure out how to deal with someone else's reactivity. More often than not, I find people with anxiety either avoid because they view emotions as conflict, or they get too involved and try to mediate the situation in an attempt to restore peace. It isn't until they realize that feeling their emotions provides a buffer of resiliency that this way of reacting begins to change.

REPRESSION

The main difference between suppression and repression is awareness. With suppression, you make a choice not to feel, while repression is an indication that somewhere along the line you blocked your ability to feel. Repression lies more in the unconscious mind, while suppression is in the conscious. This doesn't mean repression isn't trying to reveal itself. When it comes to anxiety, repression typically shows up through numbness, meaning you have a difficult time feeling emotions, even the good ones. This can feel scary for people with anxiety because it paints a story that they will likely live with the symptoms forever. Perhaps this is where the feelings of dread, being overwhelmed, and loss of control stem from.

With that said, know that at some point in your life repression may have served a purpose. If you or a loved one suffered from trauma or witnessed a horrific event, repression may have been your body's way of protecting you from unspeakable pain. This is often seen in veterans or people who were raised in abusive households.

Rather than get frustrated with your situation, consider thanking your body for loving you in that way. Part of your emotional detox journey will be giving yourself permission to heal and feel again. While that might seem like the scariest option, the C.L.E.A.N.S.E. is designed in a way to gradually heal these unconscious and conscious memories. There are elements of healing living within the fabric of all your emotions—both positive and negative. Trust the process and consider the possibility that anxiety is attempting to lead you toward healing.

INTERNALIZING AND PULLING IN

Another habit that an emotional detox will cleanse is the tendency to internalize your emotions. This means you are aware of your emotions but you choose not to show or express them, although you do think about them. The problem is that all that contemplating can lead to a lot of confusion. While you think about what worries you, you are not feeling at all; if you were actually feeling rather than worrying, you wouldn't feel so darn crummy.

The more you think, the less you feel. The less you feel, the more you react. One way I see clients internalizing anxiety is by their constant need to plan ahead. In some cases, they do this by being overly organized, putting all their ducks in a row and micromanaging every step along the way. Others hyperfocus on putting Plan B together. They like to have a Plan B in case their anxiety gets worse and they need to flee or escape a situation. The thought of being stuck is too anxiety provoking.

If you haven't figured it out already, you can't detox your thoughts by focusing on them. This will only inflate their existence. What started as a thought of fear suddenly turns into a story of being and feeling overwhelmed. This sometimes happens so quickly that you don't even know what hit you. This is all due to overprocessing rather than digesting the emotions that are attempting to surface. It is as if you sucked in (kind of like helium from a balloon) rather than released your stress. I call this a state of "pulling in."

Think of pulling in like gobbling your food. If you scarf it down, you never really taste it along the way. This increases the chances that you will overeat or have indigestion. Anxiety is similar—only instead of overindulging in food, you get caught up in your racing, stressful thoughts. This may be your style of reactivity. Following are some signs that you may be pulling your stress inward to make what is uncomfortable comfortable—that you are living in reactivity mode.

Signs You Are Pulling In and Overprocessing Your Emotions

- You experience a lot of bodily tension like neck and back pain.
- You have nightmares, bad dreams, or flashbacks.
- You obsess over details, thoughts, and conversations as a way to manage the tension.
- You secretly worry that if you let people know how anxious you are, you will become a bigger burden.
- You rarely ask for support and handle everything on your own to cover up your anxiety.
- You feel stuck in your life, and this inflates your worries.
- You take hours, sometimes days, to calm down after getting upset.

Take a moment and ask yourself how you pull in. What kinds of habits do you have that indicate you are internalizing rather than feeling your emotions? What are some ways you bottle up stress? When I ask my clients this question, they are often unsure how to respond. Many talk about overeating; others tell me they take on large amounts of work. Here are some other things people who are pulling in and reacting rather than processing their emotions have told me:

- I compare myself to others, and when I don't measure up, I try pleasing others in an attempt to make my anxiety less intense.

- I know I am stuck in my anxiety when I secretly put myself down and tell myself I am not good.

- I tell myself how behind I am and can't think about anything but my to-do lists.

- I keep busy working so I don't have to talk about anything that is bothering me.

- I snack mindlessly on food to give myself a break from feeling anxious.

EXTERNALIZING AND PUSHING AWAY

Externalizing is another way you may overprocess your emotions that can be detoxed. Externalizing emotions means voicing them or projecting them onto other people or situations. Some forms of externalizing can be healthy. Learning to communicate your thoughts and feelings in a calm and respectful way is one of the keys to living a life of good health, wholesome relationships, and emotional freedom. This is not the kind of externalizing I am discussing here.

The way externalizing leads to overprocessing is when you react to the symptoms of anxiety by consciously and unconsciously pushing your emotions away. As this occurs, you diminish the space for healing and connection. Following are some ways you may do this.

Signs You Are Pushing Away Your Emotions

- You are quick to judge, and make critical or sarcastic remarks about other people and situations.

- You make a joke when you feel tension, thinking this will lighten things up when in reality you are managing your own anxiety.

- When you are anxious you get talkative and needy for reassurance or attention.

- You are quick to apologize (sometimes repeatedly) when you feel bad, guilty, and anxious.

- You ignore feelings (including feeling anxious) for the sake of taking care of everything and everyone else.

- You report everything you do, tell people how much you have on your plate, or talk about what you had to deal with as a way to passively let people know the amount of anxiety you incurred that day.

- Compliments make you feel nervous because you don't really believe them, so you push them away by either minimizing them or ignoring them.

- You get distracted by other people's problems and may use them as a way to take the focus off your emotions.

- You are quick to snap or get upset, because anxiety makes you feel impatient and easily irritated.

I have found that people with anxiety push their feelings away because somewhere along the line they started to believe that controlling their emotions (by either pushing them away or pulling them in) would somehow make things better. If you experienced anxiety in your childhood, perhaps in the form of moments of great uncertainty, doubt, unworthiness, or fear, you may continue to feel as if you're living in those circumstances even when they're in the past. This makes you feel unsettled; so to control the discomfort you manage your emotions by never letting them close enough to be experienced.

You have probably become rather proficient at learning how to avoid your emotions—but then you inevitably learn how to push away joy as well! Perhaps this is why people with anxiety tend to be rather weak at receiving praise or taking in love and affection from others. Instead, they put their guard up and navigate their relationships, so they don't have to experience fear of rejection and/or intimacy.

Here are some other things people who are pushing away rather than processing their emotions have told me:

- I say "uh-huh" a lot and pretend I am fine, when in reality I feel numb and as if I'm going into the freeze response.

- I tend to focus on what I don't have—a partner, children, money, or freedom to follow my dreams—rather than viewing situations as things and experiences I can have. This brings on serious self-doubt and insecurity.

- When I am busy or have people to help, I feel like I have a purpose. The challenge is when those needs go away; then I am left with undigested feelings of sadness or insecurity that exacerbate my anxiety.

- I count calories or restrict food (even when I'm starving) to control my fear of gaining weight. When I allow myself to eat, I binge on things that make me feel worse, like potato chips and candy.

PERFECTIONISM

Emotions can also get overprocessed when we set the bar too high, so we will detox perfectionism as well. This means your expectations and standards tend to be unattainable. People with anxiety intuitively know that they are often capable of more than what they are currently accomplishing; however, their constant mind chatter drains their energy and weakens their skills and abilities. This can make you a little tender to receiving feedback and constructive criticism. In other words, you really feel bad or take things hard when someone gives you their opinion, even if it is clearly the result of their own reactivity. In the emotional detox journey, you will be purifying the thoughts and behaviors that contribute to the need to be perfect and discovering how that need is connected to your sense of self-worth.

You may also experience bouts of being a perfectionist if you are having anxiety over the fear of being imperfect. This makes you more reliant on external validation, or the need to have others approve of you or your work, goals, and choices. While having high standards can motivate you to reach certain goals, if you don't feel your emotions this can come at a high cost—in this case, anxiety—making it difficult for you to function in daily life.

If you are someone who volunteers for a task even when you're overwhelmed or adds three things to your to-do list for every one thing you cross off, you know what I mean when I say you're stuck in another kind of perfectionism. *Slow down.* Allow yourself to complete a few tasks on your list before adding another. Otherwise, you might find yourself in high levels of reactivity often identified through procrastination. On the flip side, you may find yourself overworked, staying up all hours of the night yet unable to meet your own standards.

Following are some indications that you might be a perfectionist.

Qualities of Perfectionism (Overprocessing)

- You ponder something so long that it makes it difficult for you to get started.
- You believe you failed before you even begin.
- You constantly wonder if someone will approve or like what you have done.
- You suffer from low self-worth and you expect more from yourself and little from others.

- You need a lot of reassurance and when you don't get it this makes your anxiety worse.

- You have trouble completing tasks and have a lot of unfinished projects, which makes you feel anxious.

- You have a hard time setting clear limits and boundaries.

- You set the bar high, and go over the top by always doing extra.

NEGATIVE NARRATING

Living with anxiety can often feel like a roller coaster ride. Life may have its ups and downs, but often the real stomach-dropping moments come from the stories you tell yourself about what is happening. People with anxiety can get stuck in wanting to predict the future. For example, they may ask me things like, "Do you think I will graduate?" or "When will I get a promotion?" When I ask them what is going on in their heads and what are they telling themselves, often I hear narratives such as, "I have no time to study and I will probably have to take the exam again" or "There are no good available men in the world" or "My boss is going to be disappointed and I might lose my job." These kinds of narratives fuel rather than soothe worried thoughts, and are likely to begin with some variation of the following:

- What if…
- I can't…
- Why…
- I will never…
- I try…
- I should…
- You always…
- You never…

The good news is that the C.L.E.A.N.S.E. method will teach you how to redirect your awareness so that you are no longer feeding this chain of reactivity. Over time this will deflate some of your negative self-talk.

These inner dialogues are so debilitating because they are influenced by the energy of undigested emotions like feelings of unworthiness, abandonment, rejection, fear, and sadness. When I dig in using the C.L.E.A.N.S.E. method, it is common for me to discover feelings of horror, terror, fear, and isolation. Once clients see the connection between undigested emotions and the quality of thoughts they are having, they pay attention to what is going on around them, question the stories they tell themselves, and recognize how they have ignored or fueled their inner struggles of anxiety.

Right now, it may be difficult for you to imagine a life without constant narration. Perhaps part of you is resistant to letting go. This is because, when left unattended, these stories merge with your identity. You can't imagine a life without them. You may be wondering who you will be, how you will act, what it is going to be like. I will tell you right now, this is anxiety and not who you really are. In fact, once you C.L.E.A.N.S.E., you are going to experience a big awakening. You will realize that on the other side of those symptoms there are positive qualities within you ready to be acknowledged and developed.

ATTACHMENT TO COPING

In the emotional detox journey, you won't be cleansing coping but rather your *attachment to* coping. Attachment happens when your coping mechanism becomes a way to manage your anxiety rather than digest your emotions. This is where detoxing can get tricky yet interesting. What I have found is that without feeling your emotions, you can unconsciously merge positive coping mechanisms (such as breathing, meeting with a friend, or a brief time-out) into the anxiety cycle.

Having coping skills is important. After all, you need them to be able to get through daily life. Without coping skills, minor stressors such as standing in the line at the grocery store might throw you over the edge. I know for me, chitchatting with another customer or reading a magazine always helps. Here is what I have learned: Coping skills work great, so long as you know they have an expiration date. This means coping (like going for a walk or pausing to meditate) is great for the short term, just until you are ready to take on your emotions themselves. Rather than needing to go for a walk to calm down, instead (after C.L.E.A.N.S.E.ing) you will go for a walk to connect to your emotions and experience joy.

Once you get through that grocery line, take a break from class, or ask someone to give you a hand at work, consider you are only partially there. At some point, it would be in your best interest to dig into whatever emotions are attempting to surface. Otherwise you might find yourself frustrated or even disappointed with the tools and strategies (e.g., taking a deep breath) you implemented and less likely to utilize them again. Instead you might choose to suck it up, will-power your way through, or develop an I-don't-give-a-damn attitude (when you know the truth is that you really do).

Actions are important, but attachment to how your actions play out probably means you were influenced by an agenda—either your own or someone else's. You know this because you might leave a situation feeling unsettled, upset, or more anxious than before. This is why cleansing is so important. As you detox your attachment to coping, you become more aware of how you might be fostering your own and other people's anxiety.

Imagine getting really upset or frustrated when you can't exercise. You tell yourself you have no time for self-care. While exercise is important and good to alleviate the symptoms of anxiety, if you are stressed or upset and ranting and raving in your head about your lack of exercise, then you are attaching to this coping. Ask yourself if an undigested emotion is coming up in you and needs to be healed. Here are some undigested emotions that could be attempting to surface:

overwhelmed, frustrated, unsupported, and overextended. While exercising gives you a boost of endorphins and other feel-good hormones like serotonin, without awareness and digestion of your emotions, those inner feelings of being unsupported may silently fester. Do both—exercise and digest—and you will be golden.

When you attach to having to cope with your anxiety, you are maintaining emotions as they are. By choosing to C.L.E.A.N.S.E. you are allowing your emotions to transform into energy, which not only detaches you from outcome but also strengthens the effectiveness of the tools and strategies you choose to put in place. In Chapter 6, we'll look at how processing emotions works.

RECAP

- Reactivity is how you make the uncomfortable comfortable.

- In an emotional detox, you clear the ways in which you resist digesting your emotions.

- You can't detox your thoughts by focusing on them.

- When you attach to your coping strategies, you inevitably make them a part of the anxiety cycle.

- The energy from the transformation of your emotions detaches you from outcome while enhancing the usefulness of your current tools and strategies.

CULTIVATE CALM

Strength is your ability to sit with anxiety long enough to allow an emotion to be processed.

CHAPTER 6
HOW EMOTIONS GET PROCESSED

"Life is 10% what happens to me and 90% how I react to it."
—Charles R. Swindoll

When you eat a piece of food, your body naturally breaks it down, absorbing what you need and excreting what you don't need. When it comes to detoxing anxiety, instead of breaking *down* you are breaking *free* from the resistance patterns and ways in which you have been controlling your emotions. Most of us have learned to view this as an active process, meaning you attempt to label or figure out what and why you are feeling the way you are, before you allow it to be digested. When I teach emotional detox, I don't exactly cut you off from this habit—instead, over the course of the process you gradually lose the need to do this.

This is because processing your emotions is an experience, not an action. Just as you might experience the incredible taste of chocolate, digesting your emotions happens when you are in a state of non-effort. You don't *try* to experience the taste of chocolate, and you don't *try* to digest emotions; you allow yourself the experience. I've found that as the experience of processing an emotion unfolds, four key elements are required: *oxygen, awareness, observation,* and *free will.* We'll look at all of them in this chapter.

Picture it like this: I can either hold a piece of chocolate and think about how much I will enjoy it, or actually take a bite and allow myself to experience the taste. If you are accustomed to a physical detox, you may be used to planning it, meaning you have to put some effort into your shopping list, deciding what you will and will not eat. An emotional detox is different. Rather than focusing on what you will *do,* an emotional detox is more about the *undoing.* Understanding the anatomy of your emotions will help, as will getting a sense of what processing your emotions feels like.

EMOTIONAL ANATOMY

While you can see, smell, and touch the food you digest, emotions are different. You can't see them (although the look on your face might reveal them) and they don't have a physical structure. Your emotions are energetic, almost electrical in nature, firing and wiring as they impact how you think, behave, and digest them. Your emotions are, in fact, chemical signals that transport information to your brain and body. As your brain receives this information (via neurotransmitters), you then have to interpret what you sense. Perceiving things as bad or threatening, as people with anxiety tend to do, produces stress hormones like cortisol, which in turn makes it more likely that you will react to rather than digest your emotions.

When these stress signals influence your neurotransmitters, it can lead to a chemical imbalance. For example, serotonin, often called the "happy hormone," sometimes is lower when symptoms of anxiety are present. Research has shown that anxiety also impacts the modulation of brain circuits and causes neurotransmitter receptor dysfunction, which can result in mental illness, epilepsy, and insomnia.

Keep in mind that your emotions are influenced greatly by memory. By design, we tend to remember events that carry strong emotions. These intense emotions often come from negative or frightening events, such as the memory of a car crash or an assault. The hippocampus of your brain is one of the areas that stores memory. Remember what I told you in Chapter 2 about the discovery of the anxiety cell? They were found at the bottom of the hippocampus—the area of the brain that influences your hypothalamus and impacts, sleep, emotional activity, hunger, body temperature, and balance. Your emotions are intertwined with *everything*, so let's start working *with* them instead of *against* them, because they have so much to offer when it comes to healing anxiety. I get so excited about this new avenue!

Let's take a moment to understand what the physiological processing of an emotion feels like by moving through a body scan.

Body Scan

1. Sit up tall with your feet hip-width apart, shoulders back and down, chin parallel to the earth.

2. Bring your awareness gently to the crown of your head. Inhale slowly (count *one, two, three*), then exhale slowly through your nose (count *three, two, one*). On inhale, you are inflating your abdomen and sides of your waist; on exhale, you are deflating, drawing your navel to your spine.

3. Lightly trace your awareness down to your chest. Allow it to rest there for a moment, then take another inhale and exhale using the same counting rhythm.

4. Move your attention to the midsection of your abdomen and gently rest your awareness there. Inhale and exhale through your nose.

5. Focus on your hips and upper parts of your thighs as you inhale and exhale slowly. As your inhale rises up inside you, allow your exhale to naturally drop your awareness to the lower half—your legs, ankles, and feet. Take a moment there and inhale and exhale.

6. Place your hands in front of your heart center, palms together in a prayer pose, and take one more final inhale and exhale.

After this body scan, you likely experienced a moment of processing your emotions, even if it was brief. How did it feel? Calm? Gentle? Nourishing? Perhaps you feel a little calmer and more centered.

You might even be thinking, *Hey, I've got this; who needs the whole C.L.E.A.N.S.E. part?* But remember that these calm processing states won't last. Why? Because there is something called triggering that happens to humans, especially anxious ones. We'll get into that in Chapter 7—first let's get to know the elements of processing emotions.

OXYGEN: TRUSTING YOUR BREATH

Oxygen is the driving force behind how your emotions are circulated, moved, recycled, and digested in your body. Because oxygen is filtered through plants and trees, our emotional well-being is integrally connected to the environment. Keeping our planet free from harsh chemicals, unnecessary waste, and toxins will mean that the air you take in is pure and clean. When it comes to processing your emotions, how you bring oxygen into your body really makes a difference. During the C.L.E.A.N.S.E., you will bring oxygen into your body through your nose (not your mouth).

Your emotions move through a process similar to the one food goes through—only instead of the amino acids and simple sugars that digest food, your emotions are digested by activating nerve channels called meridians. One of the ways to access these meridians is nostril breathing—inhaling and exhaling through your nose—like this:

- Inhale through your nose for a count of three: *one, two, three.*
- Exhale through your nose: *three, two, one.*

Did you notice an energetic shift when you did the simple nostril breathing? The process of inhaling—how you bring oxygen into your body—is vitally important to your physical and emotional health. The following steps will help ensure that your inhale is taking in the optimal amount of nourishing oxygen.

- Sitting or standing up tall with your feet parallel on the floor, slightly part your lips (so they are not pinched together). This allows your jaw to release (your upper and lower back teeth should not be touching).

- Relax your shoulders and be sure to lengthen your spine so your body does not have to work twice as hard to breath.

- Inhale through your nose, inflating your abdomen and filling in the sides of your waist as if you were filling up an inner tube. (Don't force or overdo your inhale as this may increase anxiety.)

- Gently and fully exhale and try it again.

During the C.L.E.A.N.S.E. your breathing will feel natural—some breaths will be deep while others will feel shallow. Trust that your body knows where all those undigested emotions exist and how to move them. While a shallow breath might not be "good" in your mind, it might feel great to your body. Trust...and pay attention.

AWARENESS

To digest your emotions fully and properly, you have to become aware of how they are experienced in your body. This means that you notice how your emotions show up in your body. Most often this happens through sensations. Your emotions can be experienced as:

- Overheating
- Chills
- Tingling
- Tension or tightness

- Heaviness
- Light-headedness
- Goose bumps

People with anxiety usually notice these sensations, but rather than allow them to be experienced fully, are prone to pouring reactivity on them. One of the most common ways this occurs with anxiety is through overthinking. The more you think, the less in tune you are with your emotions as bodily sensation. As a result, your body loses its ability to express itself through inner movement. This may be because you are accustomed to interpreting or judging what you are experiencing. You might find that you are quick to distract yourself from tuning in and instead focus outward.

What may be happening is that you are resisting undigested emotions that are starting to move inside you. As this occurs, it is common to experience the following sensations:

- Heaviness
- Tightness or constriction
- Bodily tension (neck pain, headaches, stomach irritability)
- Stiff muscles
- Numb or dull senses

The challenge is that the more you resist the movement (the sensations) of your emotions, the less aware you become of them. This is because resistance causes your bodily sensations to move into the fight, flight, or freeze response. When this occurs, your perception becomes clouded with reactivity. Similar to driving in the fog, you can easily go off the path of healing and become even more anxious. Suddenly you find yourself reliving your father's death, your fight with your partner, or that time in grade school when you were bullied. This retraumatization carries residue of pain from the past, causing your body to relive rather than release your emotions. The C.L.E.A.N.S.E. method is a way to remain on the path of healing and has a unique way of honoring your emotions without crossing the line into retraumatizing.

OBSERVING AND WITNESSING

While awareness is noticing, observation is the skill of witnessing. Many meditation techniques are based on learning and understanding the art of observing. According to the theory of the observer effect, simply observing a situation changes it. In an emotional detox, observing your emotions changes your experience. In other words, the emotions you once called guilt, fear, or anger now change frequency, shape, form, and movement, giving you a new and lighter interpretation that resembles joy.

To be clear, witnessing the awareness (sensations) of your emotions is different than watching. When you watch something, you are more likely to think. For example, if you are told to watch your breath, you are more likely to think about whether you are breathing "right" or "wrong." On the other hand, when you witness your breath, you are less engaged from your brain. Without awareness, watching can come from a place of surveilling or scoping out the situation, while witnessing stems from noticing and observing your breathing. While watching may be great if you are a security guard or a mom looking after small children, it won't serve you during your C.L.E.A.N.S.E. because watching is more likely to stir up old coping mechanisms, or ways you controlled and monitored (rather than experienced) your emotions.

Here is the thing: Your body is always looking to go back to a place of balance and ease. Even if you have a predisposition for staying numb, I assure you, your body is eventually going to appreciate this process. There is nothing for you to do—noticing the difference between watching and witnessing is enough:

WATCHING	WITNESSING
Surveilling	Noticing
Protecting, closed off, suspicious	Non-judgmental
Thinking or interpreting what you see	Detachment from thoughts
Being on guard	Observing without making meaning
Interacting with or attaching to thoughts	Open, curious, interested
Contracting your energy (holding in, resisting)	Expanding (allowing, opening)

Now let's apply your understanding of watching versus witnessing to the process of finding balance and ease in your body.

Finding Balance and Ease

1. Take a moment to become aware of the sensations in your body. To do this, pause, uncross your legs, soften your gaze, and rest your attention on your breathing.

2. Notice if attending to yourself in this way makes you feel upset or bothered. You might get fidgety or your heart may speed up. If so, you are probably watching or trying too hard.

3. You can help yourself transition from watching to witnessing by stating aloud the word "witness" and then breathing in and out through your nose.

4. Say the word aloud a few more times, gently speaking directly to your body: "witness" (*inhale, exhale*), "witness" (*inhale, exhale*). Keep your chin parallel to the floor and your gaze soft (looking down or along the horizon).

5. Give your body some time to adjust and align with this word. It will get there, but it might not happen immediately.

My husband and I once went to a concert. It was late and both of us were wondering when the band was going to come on stage. We chatted with people around us while we kept a close eye on the stage for any signs of new movement. Finally, around nine thirty, the band started. In the beginning, I was thinking things like *Gee, this started late; this is going to be a late night*. I also wondered about the traffic and if we ought to stay for the entire show. Suddenly, I realized I was watching the band rather than witnessing. You can tell if you are watching if you are still engaging your thoughts. To witness, I had to relax my body, take in the music, and allow myself to feel rather than think about the music.

FREE WILL

It is not unusual for me to get an email or phone message from a frantic parent. They typically start with something like: "My teen or child is suffering from anxiety and you were recommended by so and so." My response is always the same: "Let's make an appointment and see if I am the right fit for your child. Don't be afraid to shop around." While I believe that the C.L.E.A.N.S.E. will help their child, I want them to choose it.

This is because I know that free will matters. You can get a million healing treatments, spend your money on all sorts of modalities, accumulate a bunch of tools meant to help you overcome anxiety—but until you choose to heal, you may find the results you get are short-lived. Free will means choice, and in the case of the C.L.E.A.N.S.E. you are choosing whether to heal or to revisit old patterns. You are also choosing whether you pay attention to thoughts or to feelings.

If you are struggling with symptoms of anxiety, it is likely you have been giving your thoughts an excess of attention. What starts out as one thought ends up being a slew of mindless chatter. When you attend to your feelings via self-talk and negative narratives, you are choosing to use your free will against yourself. I believe that is self-sabotage.

Let's say you find yourself trembling. To cope with the shaking, you either tell yourself to calm down or you overfocus on the shaking so much that it increases to panic and your thoughts of *I am shaking* turn into *What if I throw up?* or *What if I have a panic attack?* In other words, you use your free will (choice) to focus on your thoughts as well as how you cope with them (panic). These types of thoughts and reactions could cause you to really believe things were out of control. However, what is really happening is that you have undermined the power of your own free will. As author Marianne Williamson stated in *A Return to Love*, "Our deepest fear is not that we are inadequate. Our deepest fear is that we are powerful beyond measure. It is our light, not our darkness, that most frightens us." Your free will is your light! The C.L.E.A.N.S.E. process helps you reclaim it.

RECAP

- Digesting emotions happens in a state of non-effort.
- Emotional detoxes are more about the undoing than the doing.
- There are four elements for digesting an emotion: oxygen, awareness, observation, and free will.
- Breathing moves emotional energy.
- Awareness is your ability to recognize movement (sensation).
- Observation is your ability to witness (rather than watch) your sensations.
- Free will can be directed toward self-sabotage or healing; choose healing.

CULTIVATE CALM

When anxiety casts a shadow on your future, trust your emotions to be your light!

CHAPTER 7

GOING RAW AND TRANSFORMING TRIGGERS

"What hurts you, blesses you."

—Rumi

Triggers...we all have them. You know you are being triggered when something sets you off and you can't let it go. Triggers are memories of buried emotions brought forth through current events. For whatever reason, as silly as it may be, when you're triggered the memory keeps popping into your mind. The pit in your stomach you feel when you think about going to a social event, the stomping of feet on the floor above when you are trying to sleep, or that horrible tense feeling when you feel like you did something wrong—those are all feelings of being triggered. Similar to how you might eliminate adding salt to your foods, going raw means you are forgoing engaging your triggers. This is not to say you will eliminate triggers from your life; that is unrealistic (after all, you can't control other people's stomps). However, experiencing a trigger doesn't mean it has to provoke a full-blown anxiety attack.

The reason you are triggered is because an emotion is coming up in you to be digested and gathering the energy to heal. Choose to digest and you will complete an old pattern of reactivity. On the other hand, choose to cling to or follow the triggered thoughts by reacting to them and it is likely you will increase their strength. This increases the chances you will experience the intensity of these same emotions at a later time—not necessarily with the same set of circumstances or even dance partners, but the charge you get will be similar. When you understand what triggers are and how to listen to and interpret them without reactivity (allowing yourself to sit long enough in the rawness), you will be able to move on and have a new experience altogether.

WHAT IS AN ANXIETY TRIGGER?

You might say triggers and reactivity go hand in hand. However, while reactivity is how you make the uncomfortable (distrust) comfortable (distance), triggers are signals of unhealed inner wounds. An anxiety trigger is most often recognized by accelerated thoughts. We all have thoughts—thousands of them a day, in fact. It is not the thoughts that indicate a trigger, but more so how they speed up, overwhelm, and consume your energy.

RECOGNIZING TRIGGERS

This acceleration often puts a tension in your body. You can recognize this tension by shallow breathing, negative fearful thinking, or bodily tightness. Although these signs show up early in the anxiety cycle, it is highly unlikely that someone with medium to high levels of anxiety-related reactivity will recognize them right away. This is because anxious people are often numb to these internal cues, especially shallow breathing. I can often pick this up in shallow breathers.

If you are not sure what a shallow breath feels like, simply imagining your email inbox can bring one on. Since most people who come to me with anxiety are too much in their heads to notice, in the beginning I might have to teach them about triggers by pointing out the certain words they repeatedly use, how they might be hyperfocusing on past incidents, or how they keep talking (often repeating themselves) despite the fact that their breath has gone way up in their chest. They might need me to point out how they are taking something personally or putting a lot of pressure on themselves. While this is how they follow a trigger—engaging it through reactivity—I find it is unrealistic to expect people with anxiety to notice triggers without understanding what they are first. This is why I am covering it here, before introducing you to the C.L.E.A.N.S.E.

Even acting like you have a good attitude or that something doesn't bother you could be a sign of a trigger! For example, someone who gets anxious when they are in an unfamiliar place might smile and pretend they are enjoying themselves when inside they are feeling fear and dread. You see, without feeling your emotions first, you are more apt to get yourself into situations that feel uneasy or entrapping. Once you learn that the energy of your emotions is there to help you rather than hurt you, this will all change. So, something that begins as a trigger may, over time, become a sign that something is coming up to be C.L.E.A.N.S.E.d.

> Jamie had been talking about how she had a friend at work she hadn't trusted for quite some time. Eventually, she couldn't take it anymore and decided to cut off their friendship. For a while, getting some space and distance to focus on herself seemed to work, but eventually Jamie's fears of mistrust resurfaced, only this time with a male colleague. Although the situation was different, the mental charge and intense anger felt the same.

Understanding reactivity and how emotions are processed helps reveal your triggers. Once you have a sense of what triggers look like on the outside (e.g., behaviors such as avoidance or running away), you can notice how they are experienced on the inside. Triggers may be evidenced through a sharp, tight, tense, or constricted sensation in your head, shoulders, and neck. When you are being triggered, it is likely you are feeling tight and distracted. Perhaps you ruminate over how to respond to a text, start forgetting things like appointments, get stuck in the mindset of everything being your fault, are distracted by a situation, or lose a lot of sleep over something that would seem trivial if it hadn't triggered you. This is because triggers tend to pre-occupy your energy. They do this by consuming your thoughts and repeatedly revisiting rather than releasing the emotions that need to be digested!

Your goal is not to get rid of triggers, but to learn how to interpret them. When you do, they give you valuable insight about when it is time to C.L.E.A.N.S.E. While it may seem the situation you are in is causing these emotions, most likely they were there, dormant, the entire time, because a trigger is most often a sign you have an undigested emotion from the past attempting to surface. If you didn't, then you wouldn't get so worked up. This explains why a situation can really upset one person while another is able to move on and let it go. The good news is that the triggering person or situation is letting you know that you have the opportunity to heal (move) an emotion so it can be transformed into something new.

Signs of a Trigger

- Numbness or drawing a blank
- Clenching, tightness, increased heart rate*
- Distractibility*
- Heat
- Irritability or annoyance
- Mind chatter*
- Restlessness*

- Rumination*

- Tension or tightness*

- Quickness to react

*Signs specific to anxiety.

The bottom line is that triggers are attempting to help you, not hurt you. Because you viewed it as hurt, it is likely anxiety became a way for you to control and manage your triggers. This is why it helps to stop calling what you are experiencing (e.g., tension) a symptom and start seeing anxiety as a reaction. As you do, you will notice many signs of a trigger could be interchanged with the symptoms of anxiety.

RECOGNIZING PRE-TRIGGERS

Since using this method, I have developed (as you will too) a keen sense for *early* signs of a trigger. You might even call them pre-triggers. They're usually indicated by phrases like, "I think...," "Maybe I...," "I try...," "I can't...," or "I always...".

As you become familiar with the C.L.E.A.N.S.E. method you will be able to pick up on these subtle signs early on, so they don't play themselves out in relationships or physical symptoms. Try this now:

- Sit upright with your two feet on the floor.

- Tune in to your breath, chin parallel to the ground.

- Relax your shoulders and jaw.

- Observe your breathing without labeling it as good or bad, better or worse—just notice.

- Say "I try" (or any of the phrases from the previous list) aloud.

- Observe your breathing.

What happened? Did you stop breathing? Did your breath become shallow? If you are unsure, do it again. Start from the beginning, tune in, say the word (any word on the list) aloud, and notice the impact on your breathing. There is no right or wrong. I have found many people with anxiety, for whatever reason, become shallow or hold their breath when they use these phrases. This may be a subtle sign you are in the premature stages of a trigger.

To help yourself pick up on those early cues it will be important for you to decipher the difference between judgment and discernment. The moment you go into judgment you risk following or engaging a trigger.

JUDGMENT	DISCERNMENT
Tuning out	Tuning in
Labeling ("He is crazy.")	Listening
Deciding	Observing
Discriminating	Noticing
Dissociating	Connecting

Another way to identify an anxiety trigger is when something doesn't feel right in your gut. Trust that! You might not know what emotion it is, but if you obscure this feeling with mind chatter, you might miss subtle early signs and make the trigger even more overwhelming.

TRIGGERS CAN BE ROOTED IN UNCONSCIOUS MEMORIES

While it may seem logical to focus on getting rid of those triggering thoughts and push away uncomfortable sensations, it isn't until you learn what triggers are really made of that you will be able to do so. Peel away the reactivity within a trigger, and you will find both conscious and unconscious memories. Some of these memories go back to childhood. Here is the interesting part: These memories are not only comprised of events, people, and situations you may have encountered but also *emotions that were never processed fully*. In addition, you might be picking up on other people's triggers. Yes, just as an emotion like anxiety can be contagious, so can people's triggers (e.g., tension, dread). Before you wonder how this could be, remember that it is a good thing. You want to sense and feel someone's triggers because it helps you become a less judgmental or reactive person. Picking up on triggers can also keep you safe, as they can be easily interchanged with a gut feeling, the kind of sensation that makes the hair stand up on the back of your neck when responding to danger. For example, if you stand too close to someone you might pick up some tightness in your gut. This could be an indication that you are picking up on the anxiety of the person next to you. You suddenly get a gut feeling like you ought to give them a little space. Once you do, the feeling in your stomach starts to ease up a bit.

Before you start wondering exactly which emotions are looking to be healed via triggers, I encourage you to stay within the framework of the C.L.E.A.N.S.E. This means don't go too far off track, as you could end up traumatizing (reliving) rather than completing these emotions. Sure, it could be an emotion from long ago—however, it may also be an entrenched coping mechanism. For example, if you had a parent who was a yeller or blamed others, you may have learned to cope by becoming cold or distant. On the other hand, you may have made up for this loss of energy (connection) by overfocusing on the well-being of others. Perhaps chronic worrying was a way you self-soothed or used as a way to numb your pain.

Triggers can be a form of inner guidance when they lead you to memories or emotions that need to be digested. Without awareness, though, triggers can contribute to misinterpretations.

MISINTERPRETING

As you uncover the truth about triggers, they become exposed for what they truly are—undigested emotions—and as this occurs, you become more confident and decisive in how you approach them. You learn to see that the things you may be upset about right now have less to do with the current situation and more to do with an unconscious memory. Since memories get embedded into our cells, I wouldn't rule out the possibility that just like you can inherit a predisposition for anxiety, you may have inherited a few undigested emotions. Or perhaps you had a childhood experience of being exposed to undigested emotions. This can easily happen in the formative years before you had language or maybe even in the womb!

You may be misinterpreting a trigger if you jump in quick or respond to things without taking even a nanosecond to feel first. You may act or react without the energy of the emotions to support you, using their immobility as a launchpad for pursuing or ignoring what is bothering you. This can lead to a lot of miscommunication, conflict, and harsh feelings. While getting pissed off, bent out of shape, or using the silent treatment might feel appropriate in the moment, ultimately you are likely to feel worse. This is because rather than gaining energy from your emotions, you lost energy, which inevitably increased symptoms. The purpose of triggers is to redirect you to what is happening on the inside, not to retraumatize you by internalizing what is happening on the outside. If you are being triggered, it is likely what you are thinking is not completely true. This is because you are reacting rather than transforming your emotions.

TRIGGER	TRUTH
Old wound	Undigested emotion wanting to be healed
There must be something wrong	Opportunity to heal
Limited movement of energy	Full movement of energy

The perplexing thing is, deep inside your subconscious mind, you may really believe all that worrying serves a purpose, that dwelling on your love life or your finances has an effect on them. Trust me, you're not the only one! These beliefs are typically established during childhood before your brain and body are fully developed. This creates a lot of uncertainty and possibly is due to the fact that what you have misinterpreted as an emotion was actually a trigger.

UNDERSTANDING EMOTIONAL FREQUENCIES

As you learn how to digest your raw, unfiltered emotions, you will see how digesting impacts the way energy moves in your body.

EMOTIONS = ENERGY

Your emotions are made of energy—molecules and atoms in motion. The higher the frequency, the higher the vibration. Painful emotions such as guilt or shame tend to have a lower frequency, meaning they move at a much slower rate in your body. This is why you experience heavy, unpleasant sensations (similar to what it feels like if you get kicked in the gut) along with those emotions. On the other hand, uplifting emotions such as love and joy tend to have a higher rate of inner movement, which makes you feel energized, calm, and centered. The higher the frequency, the greater the amount of relaxation you will feel.

The cool part is, when you allow yourself to feel your emotions, you can influence their level of frequency, transforming what once seemed out of control (anxiety) into hope and possibility. In other words, what you call "fear" in the beginning of the C.L.E.A.N.S.E. is likely to be transformed to frequencies of love and joy.

USE TRIGGERS AS SIGNPOSTS

When you try to stop, avoid, or get rid of your emotions, you are slowing down the process of transforming them into more pleasant, calming states. In his book *Power vs. Force*, David R. Hawkins explained that if you *increase* the frequency (rate of movement) of your emotions, you change the vibration. I've learned that this process of transformation comes with a little bit of discomfort. However, this tension dissipates when you allow yourself to feel what is happening rather than react to it. This may be in the form of tension and tightness and you may read that as a signal that something is wrong. This triggers you to think and react, which controls the vibration of the emotion. It is no different than telling your body, *nope, not gonna happen, no feeling, you go back inside*, but the only way out is through.

Your job is *not* to get rid of triggers, but to pay attention to them. Gather the information through observation, and as you do your body will digest the emotions fully (like food in your belly), giving you a boost of energy rather than creating a pit in your stomach. You may be accustomed to trying to push your thoughts away. When it comes to an emotional detox and anxiety, you will be better off if you attend to those thoughts in a new way. If they keep returning, pay attention— they might be trying to help. In the case of anxiety, those triggers are an indication of an emotion looking to be digested. So rather than running a story or narrative around what you are thinking, say to yourself, *Hey, I keep having these thoughts…perhaps my body is looking to release an emotion.*

The good news is, the C.L.E.A.N.S.E. gives you the skills to do this in a way that is not only effective but long-lasting. We often put ourselves through the wringer by thinking, problem-solving, and wrestling with our thoughts rather than looking to them as a signal for what the body is attempting to say. When you follow your triggered thoughts and turn them into repetitive worries and stories, the signals are misdirected. What you formerly referred to as "symptoms" might actually be your body's way of sending a trigger in an attempt to increase your energy so you can resolve those anxious feelings. Let the trigger point you toward digested emotions and higher vibrational energy.

WHEN OTHERS ARE TRIGGERED BY YOU

Anxiety is such an internal experience that you have probably become quite a master at hiding your feelings. While you might really believe people have no idea what you are going through, take my word for it, they know something is going on. They might not fully understand but they know something is up. They can sense your discomfort. They might be quick to assume that you are not happy or maybe they start to wonder if they did something wrong. Either way, this happens because they are starting to be triggered by your energetic frequency even more than by your behavior!

Others then try to figure out how to cope with *your* anxiety, when in truth, they are reacting to their own. After all, if they didn't have some unresolved feelings within themselves, they would be able to handle the shift in your energy with more ease. When others cope with you, this can happen in hurtful ways. All it takes is a few remarks (when you were already feeling low) to intensify those self-deprecating thoughts. You know, the ones that tell you how unsupported and unappreciated you are. It isn't until you start C.L.E.A.N.S.E.ing on a regular basis that those around you will put their defenses down. This may take time, as each of you might be used to living in reactivity.

As you learn to listen to rather than follow your triggers, people will be able to experience you in a new way. They will trust what they feel around you more so than what you do or say. You will still be the same person with your unique personality, but the difference will be that you will no longer be making faulty decisions or running on low energy.

VULNERABILITY

As you get to know your emotions in raw form, you will see it is much easier to transform them from this state. Think of it this way: The result will be much tastier and healthier if I start with a raw piece of meat and turn it into a nice meal than if I heat up something that was preseasoned, precooked, and laden with preservatives. While both may be edible, no doubt the meal cooked from scratch will be better for you in the long run.

To do this, you have to be willing to lean into (rather than away from) your emotions, especially during those moments you feel vulnerable—those times when you are ambivalent about speaking up, trying something new, or admitting you are not feeling as strong or capable as someone else may think. Vulnerability is something we all experience; the challenge is that you have likely learned how to protect yourself from it. This can show up in a variety of ways. What I see often in people with anxiety is that they keep themselves busy—preoccupied, really—so they can avoid these sensations.

Triggers make you feel vulnerable because they can occur unexpectedly. You can't control a trigger; however, you do have a say in how you respond. In the emotional detox journey, your response will be the steps of the C.L.E.A.N.S.E. As you practice listening to your body, embracing those negative, fearful, or reoccurring thoughts as opportunities rather than setbacks, this strengthens your ability to catch those subtle signs of reactivity, so that you don't have to put yourself (or anyone else, for that matter) through the wringer to get yourself feeling solid, confident, and strong again.

RECAP

- Going raw means to experience your emotions as is without going through the cycle of reactivity.

- Triggers can be a sign of old wounds held suppressed by undigested emotions.

- The purpose of triggers is to redirect you, not to retraumatize you.

- Triggers do not represent your truth.

- Some of the ways you have been coping with your triggers are reactions.

CULTIVATE CALM

Anxiety is not a sign of weakness—it is an indication that you are strong. Feel your emotions and this strength will be revealed to you.

CHAPTER 8

PREPARING FOR YOUR ANXIETY DETOX

"Ask for what you want and be prepared to get it."
—Maya Angelou

If you were preparing for a physical detox, you might begin by drinking an extra glass of water per day, cutting back on late-night eating, or gathering ingredients for smoothies. When it comes to an emotional detox, especially one for anxiety, you also need to prepare yourself. But instead of going to the grocery store, you will brush up on your intention-setting skills.

You are probably fairly good at setting goals. I find many people with anxiety are, because they spend time forecasting the future. For example, they might tell themselves they have to make money because if they don't, their car is going to break down and they will lose their job because they won't be able to get to work. As you can imagine, this type of self-talk may motivate you, but it will do so in a negative and anxiety-provoking way.

In this chapter, you will learn the value of setting intentions along with your goals, three pre-cleanse questions to ask yourself, and a new way of responding that conserves (as opposed to wasting) your energy. Maintaining the movement of your vibrations through feeling allows you to respond to yourself (and others) in a kinder, gentler way, increasing the chances that you will develop a strong sense of self-awareness as opposed to self-consciousness. We will begin by differentiating between these two things.

THE DIFFERENCE BETWEEN SELF-CONSCIOUSNESS AND SELF-AWARENESS

I used to think self-consciousness and self-awareness were in the same family, similar to how salt goes with pepper. I have come to realize they couldn't be further apart. Self-consciousness has an entirely different energy system because it feeds on self-contained emotions such as insecurity, doubt, guilt, and shame. Self-consciousness is the place where *I never*, *I should*, *I can't* come from.

You know you are operating from self-consciousness when you (re)act quickly, skip breakfast, allow how you look to ruin your day, sabotage your goals, or pay attention to those fearful narratives running in your head. To be self-conscious, you have to be more attentive to what everyone else feels or thinks about you than to how you feel or think. The challenge is, since you have no control over what other people think or do, this can lead to toxic behaviors where you act out (rather than dissolve) emotions of envy, bitterness, jealousy, and hatred.

Self-awareness, on the other hand, is where joy lives. To be self-aware means you have some knowledge about your own character, tendencies, feelings, thoughts, and behaviors. Rather than getting sidetracked by other people's stuff, you are interested in developing your own inner awareness—how your feelings impact the sensations in your body, the quality of your thoughts, and the rhythm, rate, and depth of your breath. Here are some of the differences between self-consciousness and self-awareness:

SELF-CONSCIOUSNESS	SELF-AWARENESS
Judges	Nonjudgmental
Closed-minded	Open-minded
Critical, focusing on what is wrong	Observant, open to opportunity
Triggers past wounds	Heals past wounds
Insecure, doubtful	Aware, present
Impulsive, wants a quick fix	Willing to be in the process

When it comes to your emotions, you will never, I mean *never*, be wrong for feeling them. Experiencing your emotions cannot harm you, or anyone else for that matter. However, you can do a heck of a lot of self-harm to yourself and/or your situation by overthinking (reacting).

THE THREE PRE-ANXIETY CLEANSE QUESTIONS

I have such a hard time with my ex-husband. Receiving a text from him about the kids throws my whole day off. As soon as I see his name on the screen of my phone, my heart starts pounding, my chest gets tight, and I can feel the heat building in my body. This makes me think about how much I can't stand him. I know that is not good for my kids to see. I am wondering if you can help me get rid of this hatred I have toward him.

I hear many variations of this from my clients. If you have ever experienced a strong dislike for someone or something, you know how toxic holding on to those feelings can be. Without awareness, they can spill into other areas of your life, tainting your goals with frustration and anxiety. This is why I strongly suggest that before you set your detox intentions and goals, you ask yourself the following three pre-cleanse questions and release the self-destructive behavior of going to your thoughts before going to your body.

The three pre-cleanse questions are:

1. How is my breathing?
2. How distracted am I?
3. What is the quality of my thoughts?

Here is the most important part of this training tool: *You don't answer the questions.* You simply breathe. Your answer is your inhale and your exhale. This is the beginning of learning how the C.L.E.A.N.S.E. method works. Let's go through each question one by one.

QUESTION 1: HOW IS MY BREATHING?

Answer: Inhale…exhale…breathe naturally…
Notice: People with anxiety have convinced themselves that they can't breathe, or that breathing is hard. This makes it more likely they will avoid breathing or critique themselves. After asking yourself this question, let your breath be as is. This is important—you are learning to answer with your breath, not your mind.

QUESTION 2: HOW DISTRACTED AM I?

Answer: Inhale…exhale…breathe naturally…
Notice: Again, people with anxiety tend to use these types of check-ins as an opportunity to focus on all their distractions and, in some cases, to remind themselves how they are not present. Just inhale, let your mind relax, and exhale your answer.

QUESTION 3: WHAT IS THE QUALITY OF MY THOUGHTS?

Answer: Inhale…exhale…let your breath be what it is…raw, shallow, jagged, deep…it does not matter—let your body speak.

Notice: I find people with anxiety tend to hang out in the worried, fearful areas. When it comes to an emotional detox, you will be allowing your body to settle in at neutral. Neutral says, "I can feel my emotions no matter what is happening in my life."

These three pre-cleanse questions are like training wheels. Once you get the hang of how they work, you can omit them. The timing of when to stop using them is entirely up to you. Quite honestly, depending on the amount of stress in my life, I might put my training wheels back on from time to time. For example, if I am anxious about one of my children being upset about something, the three pre-cleanse questions refocus my attention on building self-awareness.

REACTIVITY LEVELS

Another way you will know if it is time to put your training wheels back on is if you are spending time in high levels of reactivity. Notice in the lists that follow that there is no "zero level" of reactivity. This is because you are an emotional being, not a robot. You will experience emotional fluctuations in your body—that is what makes you unique and irreplaceable!

High Levels of Reactivity

- You are unaware that you are in a trigger.

- You are in the throes of the story.

- You are all worked up, highly distracted, having a difficult time holding it together.

- You aren't asking for help and are more likely to give up.

- You may cancel an appointment, quit a class, or quickly up your medication.

- You may be in conflict with others, highly defensive.

Medium Levels of Reactivity

- You are aware of your reactivity, but you are not doing anything about it.

- You have tools and knowledge but choose to suffer in silence.

- You may be avoiding others and stuffing your feelings inside.

- On the outside you look like you are okay, while on the inside you may be falling apart.

- You may be worried, forgetful, and exhausted.

Low Levels of Reactivity

- You notice the tightness and tension in your body.

- You interpret the tightness as bodily feedback and insight.

- You choose to do your three presses (see the Clear Reactivity chapter in Part 2).

- You are aware something in you is coming up to be healed.

- You respect your emotions by allowing them to be digested.

- You are kind and compassionate toward yourself.

Recognizing your reactivity is key to preparing yourself for a C.L.E.A.N.S.E. The idea is for you to try to pick up on these early signs (which the three pre-cleanse questions provide): distractibility, quality of thoughts (fearful), and absence of breath. If you don't wait until things escalate into "symptoms" of anxiety, you can catch and digest the emotions early. Doing so will decrease the chances that you will resort to old ways of reacting.

BLISS AND GETTING TO NEUTRAL

Neutral is my favorite place to be. When you are in neutral, you are feeling without attachment to having to be in a certain state (even love). Being in neutral means your life doesn't have to be perfect or dull, but it doesn't mean you have zero reaction to anything. In fact, your life can be an absolute mess and you can still feel your emotions. I find people with anxiety set the bar a little too high. They want to go from feeling anxious nonstop to being in a vibration of love and peace without pausing in the neutral space in between. While those goals may seem brave and loving, I encourage you to tone it down a notch and aim for neutral.

Don't confuse detachment and neutrality with not having empathy. This could not be further from the truth. When you are neutral, you are able to be present without joining in misery or interrupting the flow of another person's emotional movement. This is a form of empathy!

Although you may be accustomed to seeing empathy as doing something (meaning you feel bad, so you want to make someone else feel better), in truth, empathy is the capacity to understand what someone else is feeling, to be able to put yourself in their shoes. For example, I have empathy for you because I too have experienced anxiety, or I have empathy for what it is like to be in financial stress, because I too have been there. Empathy does not mean I have to feel your emotions. My understanding is enough!

When you are in neutral, you are able to listen to someone's pain while maintaining a vibrational reflection of healing. This means others can share their pain and witness their healing in you. So powerful! Now that you have that clarity as well as the emotional movement from your three pre-cleanse questions, you are ready to set your detox intentions and goals.

SETTING YOUR INTENTIONS

I have learned from working with individuals with anxiety that sometimes how you set a goal can be a form of reactivity. If you tend to be the type of person who likes to pile it on, meaning you try to tackle everything at once, you know what I mean. For example, you might attempt to deep clean your house, become a vegan, and quit smoking all in the same week. If this is you, slow down—you are going to burn yourself out before you even begin.

Goals are typically about the future, something measurable that you aim for or look to accomplish. For example, you might want to set the goal of eating more vegetables or getting more sleep. These are some things you can easily measure. Intentions support your goals. They are based on what you will do in the moment or throughout the day to support the process of reaching your end goals. So, if you are looking to eat more vegetables, your intention may be to eat one vegetable per meal. If your goal is to get more sleep, then your intention might be to shut off electronics by a certain hour on weeknights.

Since anxiety impacts so many things—food, exercise, lifestyle, relationships, work performance, finances—you can set goals in any of these areas. Everything is connected and I find once you digest the emotions around one area this impacts another. In other words, don't get too caught up in what to focus on first, next, or last. Just begin with the goal that gives you the least amount of pressure so that you don't begin from reactivity.

You'll notice how the sample goals that follow are framed so you focus on what you will increase. For example, your goal might be to ask that cute person if they are available to hang out, meet for coffee, or go out on a date. To support your goal, your intention will be what you do in your daily life to elevate your vibration and invite connection. When it comes to the C.L.E.A.N.S.E. process, it might look like making sure you are taking full advantage of all those triggers and digesting the energy of your emotions within them so you can gain the energy (confidence, strength) to go up and talk to that person.

Remember, your priority is to feel your emotions! I find the idea of getting rid of something (e.g., I want to get rid of my shyness or fear of rejection) restrains your goals and intentions from coming into fruition. The vibrational frequency of your emotions influences how you respond to your environment. I may be partial, but I am going to strongly encourage you to include the C.L.E.A.N.S.E. method as one of your intentions. My concern is that if you don't, you will have to use your willpower (which typically means brain) as opposed to the energy from your emotions. Here are some example goals and intentions you might set to support them:

LONG-TERM GOAL: MAKE MORE TIME FOR SELF-CARE

Daily Intentions

- Practice the C.L.E.A.N.S.E. method once every day.
- Give myself at least fifteen minutes to eat lunch.
- Walk in nature twice a week.
- Carry a bottle of fresh water and lemon.

LONG-TERM GOAL: ENHANCE MOTIVATION (NOTE POSITIVE PHRASING, RATHER THAN "STOP PROCRASTINATING")

Daily Intentions

- Feel (rather than resist) my emotions (C.L.E.A.N.S.E. method).
- Take three deep breaths outdoors at least once a day.
- Assign myself one to two tasks per day (e.g., pay bills, empty one drawer).
- Write down something I am strong at and post it on my mirror.

LONG-TERM GOAL: INCREASE SOCIAL CONNECTIONS

Daily Intentions

- Practice the C.L.E.A.N.S.E. method once every day.

- Make eye contact or say hello to two people per day.
- Listen without interrupting.
- Phone two people per week.
- Make time to sit with someone else during lunch.

LONG-TERM GOAL: FEEL MORE PEACEFUL

Daily Intentions
- Practice the C.L.E.A.N.S.E. method once every day.
- Visualize an image of calm daily.
- Do three stretches first thing in the morning.
- Turn off all technology two hours before bedtime.

CREATING YOUR C.L.E.A.N.S.E. ROUTINE

Now that you have practiced your three pre-cleanse questions and developed a sense for what it looks like to set goals and intentions, it is time to create a space where you will move through the steps of the C.L.E.A.N.S.E. on a daily basis.

I totally understand there will be days you either have to skip or do it in another location, but be as consistent as you can and know the formula is flexible. You may get to Step 1, do your three presses and a stretch, and then suddenly see that the dog wants to go outside or your roommate needs to talk to you. Not a big deal. There have been plenty of times I have gotten myself another cup of coffee before resuming the C.L.E.A.N.S.E. You don't want to feel like this is a job. The C.L.E.A.N.S.E. is something to enjoy, not a chore. The times I have gotten interrupted have been informative. In fact, that is how I discovered it is okay to hang out in Step 1 for a while, particularly if you are in high levels of reactivity.

SPACE

It is nice to have a consistent space for your C.L.E.A.N.S.E. practice so your body can associate this environment with gaining movement and energy. For example, I have a regular chair I sit in that is outside of the kitchen area. My body is so accustomed to gaining energy in that chair that even when I sit there outside of the C.L.E.A.N.S.E. I find I automatically start digesting my emotions. Just as your brain and body remember things from the past, they relate experiences, images, and smells with emotional flow or resistance. Think about it: If you pull up to work each day and cringe at the thought of entering the building, your body may cringe and hold back what you feel, and as a result lose energy. The C.L.E.A.N.S.E. method is a way to retrain your system to process rather than overprocess those emotions.

TIME

The other thing to consider is the best time of day for you to C.L.E.A.N.S.E. This is not to say that you won't choose to move through the C.L.E.A.N.S.E. at other times; however, consistency is important. For some this may look like a time when you are feeding your baby, sitting in your car, or even in the shower. The most important part of creating your space is making it fairly private, comfortable, and with the least amount of distraction possible.

In addition, don't wait until you are in the throes of anxiety to undertake the process—C.L.E.A.N.S.E. is a daily ritual. As your body learns to maintain rather than plow through or avoid energy (emotions), those high levels of reactivity will decrease.

RECAP

- Practice the three pre-cleanse questions.

- Understand the difference between self-consciousness and self-awareness.

- Develop your goals in language that increases energy.

- Create intentions that support your goals.

- High levels of reactivity indicate you want to continue practicing the three pre-cleanse questions.

- Develop a routine (with a certain space and time frame) for your daily C.L.E.A.N.S.E. ritual.

CULTIVATE CALM

When you allow yourself to process your emotions fully, anxiety is no longer a barrier but an avenue toward connecting you to your purpose. Your purpose is to feel!

PART 2
THE C.L.E.A.N.S.E. METHOD

IMAGINE I SERVED YOU A BIG MEAL AND THEN ASKED YOU TO GO FOR A RUN. YOU WOULD LOOK AT ME LIKE I HAD A SCREW LOOSE. YOU MIGHT SAY SOMETHING LIKE, "I NEED A FEW MINUTES TO DIGEST MY FOOD FIRST." THE SAME GOES FOR YOUR EMOTIONS. THIS IS BECAUSE TO EFFICIENTLY PROCESS (DIGEST) YOUR EMOTIONS, YOU HAVE TO BE IN A RELAXED STATE. NOT THE KIND OF RE-LAXED WHERE YOU ARE KICKING BACK WITH A COUPLE OF MARGARITAS, BUT HOW YOU SOFTEN YOUR MUSCLES SO THAT YOUR BLOOD, OXYGEN, AND CARBON DIOXIDE CAN FLOW MORE EFFICIENTLY.

THE C.L.E.A.N.S.E. METHOD DIFFERS FROM MOST TRADI-
TIONAL TALK THERAPY BECAUSE IT ENCOURAGES YOU
TO *FEEL FIRST* AND THEN HAVE A DISCUSSION. AS YOU
GAIN THE ENERGY FROM YOUR DIGESTED EMOTIONS,
YOU WILL NOTICE YOUR CONVERSATIONS REACH A
HIGHER LEVEL. THIS IS BECAUSE PROCESSED EMOTIONS
SUPPLY YOU WITH THE CLARITY AND COMPETENCE YOU
WERE YEARNING FOR, ALLOWING YOU TO TRANSFORM
ANXIETY INTO JOY AND EASE.

THE FOLLOWING CHAPTERS PRESENT INFORMATION ON
EACH OF THE SEVEN STEPS OF THE C.L.E.A.N.S.E. METHOD.
EACH STEP MAY TAKE YOU ANYWHERE FROM THREE TO
TEN MINUTES TO MOVE THROUGH, DEPENDING ON HOW
COMFORTABLE YOU ARE WITH THE STEP.

C.L.E.A.N.S.E. STEP 1
CLEAR REACTIVITY

*When you Clear Reactivity, you open the pathway
for emotional flow. This begins to detox anxiety by letting your body
know you are choosing to feel and heal what is showing up both
physically and emotionally. Instead of looking back on the past,
however, you bring yourself into the present.*

As you learned in Part 1, reactivity is the ways in which you have tried
to make uncomfortable things comfortable. In order to detox anxiety,
you first need to eliminate as much of that ingrained reactivity as possible so that you can access the actual emotions themselves.

We will be clearing reactivity using techniques that activate something called your vagus nerve. This will be your way of letting your
body know you are choosing to heal (rather than revisit) what is coming up and giving your body reassurance that it is in a safe place and
that you are committed to being present to healing. In addition, when
you press on the acupressure points I will share with you, you send this
nonverbal message to your body.

Toning your vagus nerve is an essential first step, particularly for
people with anxiety. People with anxiety are not big on surprises.
They like to have a heads-up, and when you are clear and consistent in
your approach (rather than using tools randomly), your body begins

to trust the process. When your body knows what's going to happen and feels safe, it relaxes, improving your ability to digest an emotion.

THE VAGUS NERVE AND ANXIETY

Vagus in Latin means "wandering." The vagus nerve wanders throughout your body, beginning at the base of your skull (brain stem), weaving through most of your major organs (heart, lungs, intestines), and ending in your colon. Increasing your vagal tone activates your parasympathetic nervous system, giving you the ability to relax faster after stress. The vagus nerve has two chambers:

1. One chamber (the front part of the nerve) promotes relaxation, blood flow, and reduced inflammation.

2. The other chamber (the back) can stimulate immobilization (freeze response).

Since the vagus nerve begins in the brain stem, it intersects other cranial nerves responsible for sensory processing, such as those in your eyes and ears. Perhaps this is why meditation (sensory awareness) can also tone this nerve.

Emotions are processed best in a relaxed atmosphere. You are most relaxed when your brain and gut are able to communicate most effectively. When communication is smooth, you're able to remove what you don't need (toxic reactivity) while absorbing what you do need (energy). This notion is supported in *Accessing the Healing Power of the Vagus Nerve* by Stanley Rosenberg, which is where I learned that "Eighty percent of the fibers of the vagus nerve are afferent (sensory) fibers, which means that they bring information back from the body to the brain, while only 20 percent are efferent (motor) fibers that carry instructions from the brain to the body." Because this nerve is so key to emotional processing in the body, starting the C.L.E.A.N.S.E. process by toning it makes perfect sense.

The vagus nerve was something I learned about while researching emotions. What caught my eye was how daily toning of this nerve had the potential to alleviate some of the sciatic pain I had been experiencing occasionally since giving birth to my daughters. So, even though stimulating the vagus nerve is primarily for emotional flow in Step 1 of the C.L.E.A.N.S.E., know that the benefits of toning the vagus nerve go far beyond that. Think of the presses on the vagus nerve I will show you as similar to preheating your oven. Only instead of cooking food, you are preparing to process (transform) your emotions. Toning your vagus nerve prepares you for this.

TONING AND STIMULATING YOUR VAGUS NERVE

According to the Cleveland Clinic, most people take approximately twelve to twenty breaths per minute. People with anxiety often trigger the fight-or-flight response in their body, which creates shortness of breath. The shorter your breaths, the less your vagus nerve gets toned. Undertoned vagus nerves can lead to symptoms of anxiety, poor gut/brain connection, slow metabolism, and more.

When you tone your vagus nerve, you are stimulating and revitalizing it so your communication can be clear and consistent. In the case of an emotional detox, you want your body to have zero confusion about what you are asking it to do (heal). Therefore, toning will be an essential part of your detox program. It may be a lot easier than you think—in fact, you are probably already doing it sometimes.

Since this nerve wanders throughout your body, you may be wondering the best way to stimulate it. If I asked you to stimulate your heart, you might skip around or do a little cardio jig so you could feel it pumping. When it comes to your vagus nerve, you will know you have accessed and activated it by how you breathe. Remember: Reactivity often shows up in shallow, constricted, or confined breathing. As you tone this nerve, you will notice how your body wants to take a deep long inhale, inflating the sides of your waist, followed by a nice, grounding exhale. *Ahh*. You can access your vagus nerve in four primary ways:

1. Pressing acupressure points
2. Stretching
3. Breathing
4. Humming

I'll share some more ways at the end of this chapter but for now we will focus on the first three in this list.

PRESSING ACUPRESSURE POINTS (AKA YOUR RESET BUTTON)

Think of the acupressure points I am about to share with you as your reset button. Over time, as you work with these points, they will take you out of reactivity and back into the present moment, where your emotions are processed. Try it!

- Use the two peace-sign fingers of your dominant hand to press about an inch above your navel.

- Using the same two fingers, now press to the right about an inch directly above your navel, and then to the left about an inch— those are your three acupressure points.

- I have found that people with anxiety are so in their heads that they tend to move fast, so slow down. Let yourself hold each press for the count of two before moving to the next point. Remember, you are communicating with your body, so your body needs you to take it through, step by step, until you get used to it.

I often coach clients to press their reset button when they are over-focusing on their thoughts (following a trigger) or if symptoms of anxiety are announcing themselves. What can happen is, as you slow down, your symptoms are more noticeable. This is not necessarily because you are getting worse, but because you were keeping yourself too distracted to even notice. Your body loves when you notice it and attend to it. Be kind and gentle in how you respond. Rather than panic and follow worried or anxious thoughts, redirect yourself by pressing on these points.

The second half of pressing includes connecting the points to areas on the top of your head. (Some professionals also recommend touch points behind your earlobes.)

- With two fingers of your nondominant hand, touch the back of the crown of your head while pressing the three points near your navel with the dominant hand.

- Move the two fingers on the back of your head to the middle of the crown, and continue to press the three points on your abdomen (about an inch above the navel, and about an inch apart; think Pillsbury Doughboy).

- Then bring the fingers on your head closer to your forehead while pressing the three points near your navel.

Think of your fingertips like magnets pulling and moving energy as you intentionally apply them to certain areas. As this occurs, you are directing the electrical current (your emotions) and providing blood flow between your gut and your brain. Remember, pressing pause is not about stopping your reactions; it is about releasing the emotions!

STRETCHING

Another way to stimulate your vagus nerve is by stretching your neck and spine. I recommend simply sitting or standing up tall, with your two feet hip-width apart. Bring your right ear toward your right shoulder. Notice how difficult it will be for you to clench your jaw while you do this. For some this stretch alone may be plenty. You will know because for a second you might see resistance (holding) of the breath and then you will feel how your body wants to take an inhale.

Those of you who are still having trouble stimulating your breath can try bringing your right ear to your right shoulder, and while your ear is to the right side, look out the corner of your eye, down and to the right. Hold your eyes in that position for ten seconds and then return your head back to the center of your spine. Notice if this enhances your breathing. I find with most people it does. This is an indication that your vagus nerve is alert and attentive, which is what you want it to be before moving to C.L.E.A.N.S.E. Step 2: Look Inward.

After you are able to breathe fully, I encourage you to take a deep stretch with your arms overhead, leaning side to side. Think of it as further opening the pathways for emotional digestion. You can also add a cat stretch (similar to the yoga pose), rounding your spine forward while in a chair or standing up tall with your feet hip-width apart. When you round your spine, be sure to tuck your chin a bit (stretching the back of your neck), and then lengthen (sit or stand up tall) before you bring your arms back (squeezing your shoulder blades together), while slightly lifting your chin and opening the front of your throat. *Ahh.* Your vagus nerve loves this.

BREATHING TECHNIQUES

As I've mentioned, on average people can take anywhere between twelve and twenty breaths per minute. Toning the vagus nerve will slow your breathing down, but first you have to train it. This is where mind/body disciplines such as yoga, tai chi, and meditation can come in handy, so if you are really stumped when it comes to pressing your vagal reset, know that these disciplines can help you. You can also teach yourself. Following are some techniques I recommend.

RATIO BREATHING

In this practice, you will count your breath. For example, you may inhale for two counts and exhale for two counts. It sounds like this: *inhale one, two...exhale one, two...* On inhale, you will inflate your belly (rather than your chest): *inhale one, two...* Then on exhale, your navel moves toward your spine: *exhale one, two....* This is basic breath training.

When you feel you have that down, you can include a brief holding of the breath for one to two seconds. It will look like this: *inhale* (inflate belly) *one, two...hold one, two...*then *exhale* (deflate abdomen, navel to spine) *one, two....*Ratio breathing is pretty cool because you can expand it when you are ready, moving from the one/two hold to a four/six ratio. This means you will inhale to the count of four and exhale (longer) to the count of six. By the time you get to six, your navel will not only be pressing back but lifting in and up. This is how you access the pelvic floor, which plays a big role in digesting your emotions.

PELVIC FLOOR LIFT

When you lift your pelvic floor, you are engaging the muscles you use when you have to urinate and don't want to have an accident. Kegel exercises work the pelvic floor muscles, and if you take yoga you might have heard your teacher call engagement of these muscles a root lock or *mula bandha.*

Lifting your pelvic floor is key when training yourself to cleanse reactivity. It automatically releases your jaw and it interrupts the thinking train that so many people with anxiety seem to be on. Since it is not unusual for anxiety to show up in the morning for no apparent reason at all, I recommend you incorporate this exercise in your C.L.E.A.N.S.E. As you lift your pelvic floor (particularly on exhale) you are redirecting yourself gently back to your body, giving yourself permission to digest the emotions that are feeding this pattern of chronic thinking.

If you are wondering how the jaw and pelvic floor are connected, I suggest giving it a try right now. Slightly engage your pelvic floor muscles (squeezing the muscles you use to hold your urine if you have to go to the bathroom) and notice how your back teeth release. If they don't release you may be squeezing too hard. Think of the squeeze as about 20 percent—just enough to release the back teeth. This is a good exercise to do before you fall asleep to interrupt a habit of grinding your teeth.

Our discussion of breathing doesn't end here. Later, I will touch upon some discoveries about the breath, how it heals some of those deeper, more painful emotions.

MORE WAYS TO TONE YOUR VAGUS NERVE

Acupressure and breathing are just two ways to tone your vagus nerve. Here are a few more—try those that speak to you!

1. Sit in the sun.

2. Sing or chant.

3. Gargle.

4. Drink ice-cold water.

5. Hug someone for one minute.

6. Splash cold water on your face.

7. Take a probiotic.

8. Take omega-3 and zinc vitamins.

9. Get adequate sleep and keep a consistent bedtime.

10. Meditate.

11. Dance.

12. Chew more slowly.

13. Increase fiber in your diet.

14. Tense and release muscles (e.g., squeeze fists and then release).

15. Massage your abdomen.

16. Laugh.

17. Focus on what you appreciate.

18. Visualize calming scenes, such as a peaceful vista.

19. Rest on your right side when napping or watching a screen.

20. See an acupuncturist.

TAKING STEPS

Step 1: Clear Reactivity

Now that you have read all the ways you can tone your vagus nerve, clear reactivity, and open up your emotional pathways, know that what makes this step so effective is your intention. You are not toning because you are broken, weak, or perhaps damaged. You are choosing to heal whatever is being revealed to you. Here is a snapshot of how this will look:

Morning or Evening Ritual, Example 1

Choose three ways to tone your nerve, such as:

1. Press your acupressure points above your navel (with your peace-sign fingers or an acupressure pen you can purchase online) three times in a row. Slow down; there is no need to rush this. Watch for your inhale between pressing. Allow your body to receive the inhales. With the opposite hand, direct the movement to the back, middle, and front of your brain by placing two fingers on the top of your head (back, middle, front).

2. Stretch. Try a cat, neck, or overhead stretch.

3. Meditate for one minute with your eyes closed as you observe your body and breath.

Morning or Evening Ritual, Example 2

1. Begin your morning folded into Child's Pose. From your hands and knees, sit your hips back on your heels and

place your forehead on the floor (i.e., fold on top of your thighs with your arms down by your side). Your spine will be rounded, stretching your back.

2. Turn over and rest on your back. Do your three presses with your dominant hand while the other hand presses points on your head (back of crown, middle, and toward the front). You can place your legs in a butterfly position to open up your inner thighs (which can help your emotions flow).

3. Close your eyes for one minute, meditate, and observe your breathing before moving on to C.L.E.A.N.S.E. Step 2: Look Inward.

RECAP

- Clearing reactivity means toning (stimulating) your vagus nerve daily. When it comes to anxiety, the shortness and shallowness of your breath is likely related to an untoned vagus nerve.

- Rather than tell yourself to stop thinking or reacting, instead use your reset button.

- Practice getting to know how to access your vagus nerve with morning and/or evening rituals.

- Once you get familiar with toning, you may choose the variation that fits best with your lifestyle. For me, with three kids, it is sitting in a chair doing my acupressure presses.

CULTIVATE CALM

When you tone your vagus nerve, you redirect your awareness back to the present moment, where anxiety cannot live.

PART 2: THE C.L.E.A.N.S.E. METHOD

C.L.E.A.N.S.E. STEP 2
LOOK INWARD

When you Look Inward, you state an "I feel" sentence aloud and then answer the question with your breath. This continues to detox anxiety by loosening up the emotions you have buried without repeating their story.

I stumbled upon the Look Inward step accidentally while my husband and I were in couples therapy. At that point, we had been attending therapy for quite some time following my husband's infidelity. While we had made great gains, we both felt like the last few sessions had left us feeling anxious and stuck. Mind you, I was simultaneously researching emotions, so while the therapeutic process was helping us heal and gain skills, there was also a part of me that was beginning to see another approach—the emotional detox—emerging.

During our last therapy session, the therapist asked us how we felt about something and, for whatever reason, got distracted, moved out of her seat, and attended to some paperwork. Since she was no longer sitting in front of us, I had thirty seconds to take a deep breath. She returned to hear our answer, but it was too late—I had gone to another place, and Step 2 was born.

ACCESSING BLISS

Unlike other days when I had taken a step back to pause and breathe, that day in my therapist's office was different; it wasn't about controlling or managing my emotions. Rather than search for the answer in my head, I allowed myself to experience the answer in my body. I did so by breathing into it. I felt something I had never experienced before: an inner movement that was so impactful and peaceful I no longer wanted to disrupt the process with talking. When the therapist sat back down to hear what we had to say, I felt like I was pulled from another world, one where I felt bliss and healing. I did not want to leave this state or spoil it with useless chatter by discussing something I could not control or change. In that moment, I felt peace and I decided my path from that time on would not only look different but *feel* different.

"Are you sure you want to quit therapy?" my husband asked. "Yes, I am sure," I replied. Here is the thing: I didn't see it as quitting. I felt like it was a graduation. Something shifted inside me. I couldn't explain it, nor did I fully understand where and how I was getting such internal strength. But for the first time in my life I trusted how I felt rather than listening to what others (even the experts) said. This for me was newfound freedom.

RELEASING THE SUBCONSCIOUS

Think of your subconscious mind as a storehouse of memories that includes images, vibration (feeling or lack thereof), sensations (smell, etc.), and even coping mechanisms (how you responded) related to the emotional experiences you have encountered throughout your lifetime. In most cases, you aren't aware that you carry these memories around in your subconscious mind—though they might perk up here and there, especially when you are alone or have some serious downtime. Perhaps this is one of the reasons anxious people like to stay busy.

After years of studying and taking multiple courses in quantum physics and healing, I learned that just because you can't see something, or there is no physical evidence of it per se, doesn't mean it doesn't exist. In other words, just because something isn't on your mind right now, doesn't mean there aren't some things on a deeper level that you need to detox. No worries; Step 2 will dig them up for you.

I don't want to discredit therapy, as it can no doubt be a tremendously transformative experience. However, the lesson I learned that day in the therapist's office, and have since implemented into my work with clients, is that you can cross the line from the therapeutic process being a productive experience to it being a counterproductive one. Without awareness, you go from releasing an unconscious, buried emotion to revisiting it (replaying it). It looks something like this:

RELEASING (DIGESTING)	REVISITING (OVERPROCESSING)
Expressing your feelings	Explaining your feelings
Processing feelings	Projecting feelings
Experiencing your feelings	Investigating feelings

This is key: Notice how in the releasing (digesting) column, you can't have any of those experiences without actually *feeling* something. Also, remember that to process an emotion you need to bring oxygen *into* your body. That's why I felt so different when I allowed myself to inhale fully into the experience at the therapist's office. When you project, explain, or analyze your emotions you are unconsciously telling your subconscious mind that you are choosing to revisit rather than heal.

The second step of the C.L.E.A.N.S.E. method (Look Inward) gives you the best of both worlds. You get to voice yourself through an "I feel" statement and access subconscious buried emotions by choosing to answer with your breath. By doing so, you develop what I call your breath story. The "I feel" statement I use most often is: "How I feel in my body right now is _____."

BREATH STORIES

Your story is important because it includes what you have been through, how you have learned to view the world the way that you do, and even how your body has spoken through symptoms of anxiety. While at times it may feel different and even awkward to express your story through breathing, stay with it. As you inhale and exhale, your emotions circulate, and through the essence of sensations your story begins to be told.

In Step 2, you will begin with a "stem" sentence, state it aloud, and follow it with an inhale and an exhale. (A stem sentence is simply a prompt you'll use to Look Inward and spark your breathing exercise.) You may be wondering what kind of inhale or exhale you should practice, meaning should it be long, short, quiet, or pronounced? The only thing I would encourage you to do is inhale and exhale through your nose. Otherwise there are no hard-and-fast rules in this step. This is because some of the stories you have are represented with a shallow breath (perhaps only reaching the upper clavicles of your chest or your throat area) while other stories rise up from deep within your abdomen. I say let go of right or wrong and let your story unfold naturally, breath by breath.

My experience with clients is that shallow breathing often includes stories of grief, loss, and abuse. When I hear a shallow breath story, I know there has been great pain in that person's life. Longer inhales combined with shallow exhales can sometimes illustrate a story of struggle, feeling trapped, or insecurity. Overexhales (longer exhale than inhale) can sometimes be a sign that someone is in a constant state of coping. Their breath story tells me their life has a lot of unpredictability and they have a hard time feeling safe.

It is not our job to judge or analyze each other's breath. If anything, listening to client breath stories has taught me the beauty of patience and that if we allow ourselves to tell our breath stories first (before talking), the process will be richer. Through the development of your own breath story, you too will become more in tune and compassionate with others. With each breath, your reactivity continues to be released, allowing your pure, raw emotions to emerge. No need to worry about those, because Step 3 soothes anything that comes up.

LOOSENING ATTACHMENTS

I have learned that people with anxiety tend to resist breathing because they are attached to what may or may not happen if they experience their emotions. In the world of anxiety, you feel screwed either way. If you ignore your emotions, they will likely build up inside you, wreaking havoc on your nervous system and inner organs, which can lead to bodily inflammation. On the other hand, letting them loose may make you feel out of control. You may think *How will I handle what comes up? Will it get worse?* and *What if letting my emotions out puts me through all the anguish again?*

Loosening attachments to what could happen begins with alleviating some of the pressure you have been putting on yourself. Here is the thing: The out-of-control feeling is a reaction, not a feeling; if it were a feeling, you would not be so caught up in your head. Breathe. Your reactions (not your feelings) are what make you feel toxic.

Think of the following "I feel" statements as a way to deflate and discharge the compulsion to hang on to what is familiar (resistance) even though it is slowly contributing to your inner deterioration. Here is how it will look—give it a try. Read each (slightly different) statement aloud and allow your breath to answer, just as you did with the three pre–anxiety cleanse questions in Chapter 8.

- How I feel in my body now is _____ (*inhale...exhale...*).

- Being in my body now makes me feel _____ (*inhale... exhale...*).

- How it feels to be me right now is _____ (*inhale...exhale...*).
- Having this experience now makes me feel _____ (*inhale... exhale...*).
- Being in this situation makes me feel _____ (*inhale... exhale...*).

After moving through each sentence, it is likely you noticed how inclined you were to answer the question with your head. This is because you have been conditioned to react to (think about)—rather than experience—what comes up. The challenge with living your life in this way is it preserves your ego, which is holding you back from further progress.

DISSOLVING EGO

Your ego is your false identity. It is the one that tells you that you are an anxious person. People get defensive when I say a false identity has told you that, because it challenges what they have been telling themselves for a long time. I am well aware that saying you don't have anxiety can feel like an insult and like I don't believe or validate what you are going through. The reason I can be so bold is that I too was diagnosed with anxiety, and for a while that label seemed to get me the support I needed. What I eventually learned is that to move in a healing direction, I had to be willing to relinquish my attachment to this label. When I did, not only did it put me on a healing path but it saved me tons of time and money. My hope is to do the same for you.

When you say, "How I feel in my body right now is _____" and answer the question with your breath, you are dissolving the ego. This is because you are consciously developing the skill of Looking Inward and bringing up your feelings without rehashing or reiterating the labels and narratives. The thing is, the ego loves labels because they keep you exactly in the same place. It feeds off fear through control.

The ego does not want you to know how powerful your emotions are. It purposely keeps you preoccupied in your head so you won't be tempted to breathe. Each time you state "How I feel in my body right now is _____" and breathe, you are loosening your attachments to identifying with anxiety while overcoming your concern with outcome.

SPEAKING IN THE PRESENT TENSE

In Step 2, I encourage you to frame your statements in the present tense, even if the thing you are choosing to C.L.E.A.N.S.E. happened in the past. This is because all healing begins in the now. This is why the statement includes: "How I feel in my body right now is _____."

When it comes to anxiety, you might be accustomed to managing it from your head, contemplating the past or drifting off into the future. Part of retraining your system to *feel again* is to select language that encourages you to be in the now. With that said, keep an open mind and trust your instincts. If your statement includes a word from the past (e.g., "How I *felt* in my body when..."), it won't hurt you, nor does it necessarily mean you will regress; you just might not get as much inner movement as you would if you had taken a second to change the language to the present tense.

To help you fully understand the difference, let's take a moment and do a little exercise. The following table includes six stem sentences; three are written in the past tense and three are written in the present tense.

- Read the past-tense sentences in the left-hand column, answering with your breath (*inhale...exhale...*).

- Then read the present-tense sentences in the right-hand column, also answering with your breath (*inhale...exhale...*).

- Notice where your inhale or exhale originates (abdomen, chest, throat).

- Notice the quality of your breath (shallow, rigid, slow, deep, smooth). Just notice.

PAST	PRESENT
How I felt in my body when...	How I feel in my body now...
When I was in my body it made me feel...	Being in my body now makes me feel...
What it has been like to be me is...	Being me now makes me feel...

It is likely you experienced a different response in the amount of movement (sensation) in your breathing by reframing the question to the present moment. When you spoke in present tense, your breath might have been more engaged, meaning your inhale may have had more volume or your exhale more depth (navel to spine).

You may be wondering why. Here is the thing: When you frame things from the past, you are more likely to replay them, not just in your mind (thinking) but also in your body (feeling). The same would occur if you overfocused on the future. If you really want to heal inside and out, on a conscious and subconscious level, it is essential that you practice using language and thoughts rooted in the now.

Step 2 does poke at your past without getting into it. So, if you are feeling irritated, annoyed, or frustrated by Step 2, I say good! This is the whole point of the process of looking inward—you want to dig up all that toxic reactivity. Again, the third step is going to soothe and move everything, so let it rip.

HONORING THE WISDOM OF THE BODY

You may notice your reactions through your thoughts, but often these signals are shown through the physical body as well.

I once went on vacation with my extended family. There was so much reactivity around me, I made a point to practice the C.L.E.A.N.S.E. daily. I would take my yoga mat, plop it in the prettiest, quietest place I could find, and begin the practice. While in Step 2, I noticed something I had not noticed before. After each "How I feel in my body right now" statement, my tongue was pressing on the roof of my mouth. My sense was that this new set of circumstances was bringing some important information to me about my healing and the C.L.E.A.N.S.E.

I decided to repeat the same stem sentence three more times, following every one with a breath. When I did, each time my tongue remained pressed on the top of my mouth. Since I had written a book called *Mantras Made Easy*, I knew that when you recite a mantra, you should tap your tongue on the roof of your mouth as a way to vibrate the hypothalamus in the brain. One of the many functions of this part of the brain is to regulate emotions. To honor the wisdom of my body, I continued on to Step 3, allowing my tongue to press in this way. By the end of the C.L.E.A.N.S.E., I felt neutral, and my tongue was resting on the bottom of my mouth.

Try it! Be conscious of your tongue as you repeat: "How I feel in my body right now is _____."

TAKING STEPS

Step 1: Clear Reactivity

- Tone vagus nerve (three presses, cat/cow stretch).

Step 2: Look Inward

- State the following stem sentences aloud to yourself, following each with your breath. Remember that your breath is the answer, not your brain.

- How I feel in my body right now is _____ (Answer with your breath: *inhale...exhale...*). (Repeat three times.)
- When I care for myself it makes me feel _____ (*inhale...exhale...*).
- Not caring for myself makes me feel _____ (*inhale... exhale...*).

RECAP

- Access toxic reactions through your "I feel" statement.

- Always begin with "How I feel in my body right now is..."

- Allow your breath to answer, not your brain.

- Develop your breath story.

- Notice any tension, irritation, and/or muscle constriction.

- Know that it's okay if Step 2 brings up intense emotions (no worries; Step 3 soothes).

- Notice your tongue.

- Repeat stem sentences and breath when tension is high.

CULTIVATE CALM

Anxiety was the message and your emotions are the answer!

C.L.E.A.N.S.E. STEP 3
EMIT

When you Emit, you produce a sound in the form of a mantra: hum. This continues to detox anxiety by creating a current of energy inside you, uplifting the emotions triggered by your present situation. The hum transforms the emotions into higher states of consciousness, creating an overall cleansing and soothing effect on both mind and body.

A couple of years after I wrote *Emotional Detox*, my husband and I gathered at the Arlington Street Church in the heart of Boston. We were there to hear the great musician Krishna Das. Since most of his music was in Sanskrit, my husband didn't feel comfortable singing along, so I told him to hum. After all, the word "hum" itself is a mantra. I explained, "Mantras are sounds, syllables, or words that are repeated, and the sound *hum* actually means "enlightenment."

It didn't matter; his Irish Catholic roots kept him in check. While I stood up with my hands in the air, chanting along, he sat by my side, closing his eyes and listening. Quite honestly, this would not be the first time he would see me praising and opening my heart to something greater. Before his affair, he may have raised a hairy eyebrow at me or even warned me about what I may be getting myself into, but this had changed. Although we didn't attend our little Episcopalian church as often as we would have liked, in many ways our religion became one of forgiveness, and the sacred vibration we experienced that evening showed us how viable this frequency is.

PRODUCING

In your emotional detox journey, you too will receive the blessing of getting to know your innate natural ability to take in and produce healing sound. You will see that sound isn't just a noise but also a conduit of emotional energy. As you create the sound of the hum in Step 3, you are not only teaching your body how to regulate an emotion but also how to transform the bodily makeup of the emotion from one vibration (fear) to another (freedom).

You may be accustomed to attempting to release anxiety by zooming in on your fearful thoughts. The challenge is that as you focus on your anxious thoughts, you are more likely to turn to old coping strategies like comparing yourself to others, complaining, or self-criticism. Simply identifying your emotions isn't enough; you need to increase their inner movement so you can vibrate from higher consciousness. Anxiety was, is, and always will be a reaction to non-movement of your emotions.

When I was a kid, I remember my mother always complaining about my father. I worried she was going to teach me to hate men and I didn't want to be like that. Through the C.L.E.A.N.S.E. method, I discovered that complaining was how my mother coped with her anxiety. Much to my chagrin, I had taken on some of her tendencies. Although I was reluctant to say how I felt aloud, in my head, in the past, I would complain about my husband. This was no different than what I observed. The hum helped me free myself from some of these self-destructive patterns and move to a place of joy.

You too will learn that you can't release something by focusing on it. You can, however, transform lower-vibration emotions such as sadness, guilt, and fear into higher-vibration emotions such as love, joy, and peace. You have the tools inside you. Your hum in Step 3 will allow you to generate a greater vibrational frequency than the one that you produce when you overprocess, overfocus, and overanalyze. This is the key to the C.L.E.A.N.S.E. process.

THE POWER OF SOUND

The healing power of sound can be traced through the history of all cultures. Sound has been built into ceremonies such as weddings, funerals, and other celebrations as a way to invoke feelings of joy and to honor the significance of life. Sound touches your heart, giving you permission to sink into your soul, releasing whatever is pent up inside you. Through sound, you can create an inner rhythm between your brain and body.

Anxiety disrupts any sense of inner balance. You now know that chronic thinking dilutes and, in some cases, clogs up the communication between the brain and body. Through something called brainwave entrainment—often seen in meditators—you can rewire your system to create a steady stream of movement, which eventually will surpass the threshold of fear and anxiety. Brainwave entrainment isn't without its skeptics, but there is research to support it. In 2008, *Alternative Therapies in Health and Medicine* published a review of twenty studies of brainwave entrainment and patient outcomes. The conclusion was that brainwave entrainment is an effective tool to use on cognitive functioning deficits, stress, pain, headaches, and premenstrual syndrome. The studies also suggest that sound work can help with behavioral problems.

As you practice your hum, you will develop a sense of how sound travels through your body, how it tingles. You will also develop an appreciation for the hum as you experience the benefits and the many variations of how to use the hum, explained further next.

THE HUM

When putting together the C.L.E.A.N.S.E. method, I always knew sound would be an essential part of the formula. The question was, which sound would it be? Originally, I chose the sound *hum* because unlike the sound *om*, which is familiar to many of us through yoga, *hum* wasn't attached to any specific religious or spiritual practice. I wanted the C.L.E.A.N.S.E. mantra to be one that could be universally accepted regardless of background, culture, or religious beliefs.

Hum seemed the least threatening and most familiar. The humming sound is evident in nature (e.g., bees buzzing), it's innate in babies as they learn to vocalize, and it's one of the most natural ways you might sing along to your favorite tune. In *Emotional Detox*, I discussed the benefits and significance of sound waves. It wasn't until after the book was published that I stumbled upon further research to validate just how extraordinary the hum is.

BENEFITS OF THE HUM

Jonathan and Andi Goldman's book *The Humming Effect* solidified it all for me. The authors discuss the work of Anthony Holland, a professor and musician-scientist at Skidmore College who reputedly destroyed cancer cells and bacteria using high-frequency vibration. *The Humming Effect* lists dozens more benefits from the hum vibration, including:

- Enhancing focus and memory
- Fostering relaxation
- Lowering blood pressure
- Reducing migraines
- Reestablishing the natural rhythm of our organs
- Stimulating the thyroid gland
- Toning the nervous system

The hum even increases nitric oxide in the body. The American Association for the Advancement of Science named nitric oxide "Molecule of the Year" in 1992 for its extraordinary benefits, which include regulating blood pressure, dilating blood vessels (so your nutrients can be delivered efficiently), killing off foreign invaders to the immune system, improving sexual function, and more.

MAXIMIZING THE HUM

This technique may be one of the simplest tools you will ever come across, but here are a few guidelines to follow:

1. Remember to sit or stand up tall when you hum. Similar to taking a deep breath, if you are hunched over, sitting askew, or tilted, your diaphragm might be squished, impacting the quality of your hum.

2. Have your feet and hands uncrossed. It is ideal if your feet can be planted on the floor to ground your body.

3. Notice if you are wide-eyed; if so, soften your gaze by blinking a few times and looking down at the floor a few feet in front of you. As you gaze at the floor be sure to keep your chin parallel to the earth. This is so your neck (which is part of your spine) stays nice and straight and your shoulders are moving back and down.

HUM VARIATIONS

There are two variations of the hum that I teach; try both!

1. In the first variation, begin by inflating your lungs with an inhale, and then on exhale, chant the sound *hum*. Begin with your mouth open and slowly let your mouth close as you complete the sound.

2. In the second variation, you inhale through your nose. Then, on exhale, close your mouth right away and hum the entire time with your mouth closed. You will feel the vibration on your tongue and the roof of your mouth.

Either way, do your best to extend your hum as long as you can (until your navel is pressed toward your spine). You will know you are at the end of your hum because you will be lifting your pelvic floor (the muscles you use to hold your pee). Between hums, be sure to allow your inhale to inflate your lungs before moving into the next hum. I typically hum a minimum of three times in a row. With that said, one is better than none, and if you chant more than three that is great too. The hum will never hurt you.

DIRECTING SOUND

The other cool part of the hum or any healing sound that is repeated is that you can direct sound toward certain areas of your body. For example, if you were experiencing pain in your lower back or tension in your face, you might inhale and exhale the sound *hum* while focusing your attention on your lower back or face area. If you're not used to making sounds like this, the hum might seem silly; that's okay. If you keep practicing you'll soon see the benefits of this simple activity. Try this exercise:

1. Take a moment to sit up tall in preparation for your hum.

2. Place your hands palms-down on your lap with your fingers loose.

3. Close your eyes and place your attention on your right thumb.

4. As you are breathing simply notice without judgment the sensation of your right thumb. It is likely that the feeling in your right thumb will become more pronounced.

5. On the inhale (through your nose), inflate your lungs.

6. On exhale, chant *hum* while focusing on your right thumb.

7. Try it a few times. It is likely that you will notice the sensation increases, maybe even throbs.

As you learn to direct the energy of your hum to different areas of your body (e.g., heart, lower back, etc.), essentially what you are doing is exercising your free will to intensify movement in a certain area. This is a kind, loving gesture. Here is the thing: You cannot dislike your body and C.L.E.A.N.S.E. at the same time. When you produce and direct your humming you are choosing to give yourself everything you ever needed and did not get. For example, if as a child you needed someone to listen to you, tell you everything was going to be okay, or protect you from harm, this is your chance to give it to yourself. Do that for yourself now; don't wait for someone or something else to give it to you. Healing is never outside of you. You won't find it in a drug, a person, or a thing. Let go of trying to make it happen. There is no "it." Reframe that "it" to "is" right now, hum, and give yourself everything you already are (vibration). Yes, you really are that powerful!

INNER SPACE

As you develop your hum, you will notice you are able to hold your attention inside your body longer. When it comes to reactivity, it is likely you have been trained to go outside of your body. Even the idea of thinking about or labeling an emotion can temporarily suspend you from that inside space.

When I work with clients, I often have to wean them off this tendency. While in the beginning we might spend some time identifying some emotions over time, I guide them to hold the space inside longer, to move through what is showing up rather than be quick to want to understand and contain it through labeling. I am not against labeling; however, I suggest moving through the formula first to be sure you are not reinforcing a reaction. This is important: The hum is powerful and will inflate what you put your attention on; therefore, you will want to put your attention on what you are working toward, rather than on a person or situation that is bothering you.

Your inside space is where the energy of your emotions gets transformed. Read these instructions and then put this book down for a second to try it right now!

1. Sit up tall, feet flat on the floor, and relax your shoulders and face.

2. Keep your chin parallel to the floor and your gaze soft. On the inhale, inflate your abdomen and the sides of your waist. On the exhale, open your mouth and *hu-uuu-umm*.

3. For the first half of the hum your mouth is open and for the second half it remains closed. Feel the vibration in your mouth as you pull your navel toward your spine.

4. Pause and allow your in-breath to come in naturally and fill up your abdomen, chest, and throat.

5. Close your eyes and observe your inside space: the rhythm of your breath, sound, sensation, and tingly movement within and around your body.

6. Notice any waves of relaxation, muscles tensing then softening. Notice how your neck may want to stretch side to side and how your jaw naturally releases.

CROSSING BARRIERS

After your hum, you may notice your inhale has more volume. This is because chanting the hum encourages you to release an exceptionally long exhale. When you breathe this way, you are tapping into your cellular memory. This means as you change the frequency of your emotions, you alter the frequency of your cells, including the ones responsible for cellular memory. Since anxiety cells have been primarily located in the hippocampus (the memory storage area of the brain), altering the frequency of your cells transforms what you may have been predisposed to (i.e., heredity).

While anxiety may have gotten you to believe you were stuck or your hope for living a life with more freedom and ease was stifled, this is simply a reaction to old ways of thinking. Let the hum loosen them. Trust that it can alter the neurological patterns of anxiety. I am not saying it will happen overnight; however, with your commitment and trust you can reduce high levels of reactivity to medium levels and eventually to low levels. However, wanting it to happen immediately is a reaction, something to C.L.E.A.N.S.E., and since it is coming up now, let me show you how this works using Steps 1, 2, and 3.

TAKING STEPS

Before you begin, think about how reactivity is showing up for you at this moment. Then observe without judgment any labeling of your thoughts. Finally, conduct an assessment of how your physical body feels now.

- Reactivity communicates (e.g., thoughts of how this is going to take a long time)
- Your labeled thoughts (e.g., doubtful, reluctant, nervous)
- Bodily feedback (e.g., tension, thinking, non-movement)

Step 1: Clear Reactivity

- Tone your vagus nerve:
- Sit up tall, feet hip-width apart, arms uncrossed. Stretch your right ear toward your right shoulder, and set your gaze to the right on the floor (as if you are trying to look over your shoulder).
- Hold the gaze for ten seconds, lift your head back to center, inhale, exhale (naturally).
- Take your left ear toward your left shoulder, set your gaze to the left (peering out of the corners of your eyes), hold for ten seconds, sit upright, and allow your inhale and exhale.
- Press your three vagus nerve acupressure points above your navel (one inch above, one inch apart) three times in a row.
- Sit up tall and breathe.

Step 2: Look Inward

- How I feel in my body right now is _____ (*inhale... exhale...*).
- Being in my body right now makes me feel _____ (*inhale...exhale...*).
- Moving through the process makes me feel _____ (*inhale...exhale...*). If needed, say this two more times.
- Allow discomfort or tension to surface (e.g., tight lips), then proceed to Step 3.

Step 3: Emit

- Hum three times:
- Sit up tall, feet flat on the floor. Inhale through your nose, and on exhale *hum* as your navel presses toward your spine.
- At the end of your exhale, pause and observe your inside space. Allow your body to naturally release tension. Know sometimes things get tighter before they release. *Ah*...you are ready for C.L.E.A.N.S.E. Step 4: Activate Joy.

RECAP

- In Step 3, you learned two variations of the *hum* mantra.

- Humming is a tool that can offer numerous health benefits.

- Reciting *hum* improves brainwaves and cellular memory.

- Use your hum to strengthen your ability to remain within.

CULTIVATE CALM

Anxiety may have been the voice of your mind, but your emotions are the voice of your heart and your hum will be the voice of your spirit.

C.L.E.A.N.S.E. STEP 4
ACTIVATE JOY

To Activate Joy, you visualize an image of the qualities you are choosing to cultivate. These are likely the opposite of how you have been feeling or reacting. Activating Joy detoxes anxiety by aiming the vibration from your hum to the feeling you want to instill within you.

My client Jim suffered with anxiety due to his chronic liver disease, which caused him to miss work for various medical appointments and episodes of pain. When he had time off, he usually called his mother. While at first this seemed like a good idea, he often got off the phone feeling more drained. After guiding Jim through the first three C.L.E.A.N.S.E. steps, I encouraged him to aim the energy of his hum toward an image of feeling energized, healed, and peaceful after speaking with his mother. Because Jim had allowed himself to process his emotions with the first three steps, he was able to do so. Anchoring these images energetically into his body would follow with the next few steps.

LEARNING TO DIRECT YOUR ATTENTION

Once you complete your hums in Step 3, Step 4 teaches you how to activate joy by directing your attention. If you are experiencing symptoms of anxiety, it is likely that you are accustomed to tuning in to non-movement of emotions. This means you tend to hover over what isn't working instead of what is. For Jim, this meant he would end his conversations with his mother focused on his aches and pains. His thoughts would also dwell on his mom—the way she insensitively talked about herself while he suffered in silence.

This is where this process gets fascinating. Often, once the thing that is bothering you (in Jim's case, his mother's insensitivity) is moved through the C.L.E.A.N.S.E. steps, it transforms into a quality that you are looking to evolve within *yourself*. Jim wanted his mother to be less self-centered and more sensitive to his needs. When he visualized sensitivity, he discovered he needed to be more sensitive to his *own* needs. The things that bothered him about his mother reflected what he had to develop within himself to heal! *This is a game changer*—the thing that you may have been judging, preventing, holding back is exactly what you need to evolve.

Because of this ability to redirect awareness, the emotional detox journey and C.L.E.A.N.S.E. process has redefined how I see joy—as *a state of expansion*. Joy is when you see things in a new way that changes you from the inside out. Joy has a ripple effect, a positive and healing impact on everyone around us.

Joy can't be taught; it is not a mind thing. You can't will yourself into joy, but you can feel it. There are, however, some ways to strengthen your ability to connect to joy. That's what the Activate Joy step does! You will learn the value of visualization, the difference between joy and happiness, and what it means to live in divine time and to believe in your own energy.

TRANSITIONING FROM STEP 3 TO STEP 4

As you arrive at Step 4, you have cleared reactivity, toned your vagus nerve, made some "How I feel in my body right now..." statements, tuned in to your breath story, and belted out a few hums. It is highly likely you have considerable emotional energy stirring and moving inside your body, creating a variety of sensations. You're ready to channel joy!

When you have energy vibrating at high levels, it is important that you put your attention on the qualities you would like to strengthen. For example, if you are concerned about someone's drinking and want to say something but don't know how to help, your visualization might be one of connection, strength, and healing. Or maybe you have to give a talk and public speaking makes you anxious? If so, visualize what would make you feel safe and at ease within the group you are speaking in front of.

While I believe it is important to seek support about important issues, when it comes to your C.L.E.A.N.S.E. I recommend visualizing connection. The idea is to get you *feeling*. All too often, people overthink and focus on the discomfort. This causes you to zoom in on the thing that is making you feel toxic and anxious.

CHAKRAS

Since anxiety can impact you on both physical and mental levels, it is important that your C.L.E.A.N.S.E. include practices that can support you in both areas. If you are having trouble seeing and experiencing joy, part of supporting your activation in Step 4 is to restore balance via your chakras, which are vortexes of bodily energy connected to your organs and glands.

Information about chakras can be found in Chinese medicine as well as Hindu and Buddhist texts. It is not unusual to hear about chakras in a yoga or martial arts class. People trained in energy healing modalities such as Reiki often focus on the main chakras in the body, which run from the base of your spine to the crown of your head. When one of these energy centers is sluggish or blocked, it is said to contribute to both physical and mental ailments. There are seven main chakras—crown, third eye, throat, heart, solar plexus, sacrum, and root—but for the purposes of cleansing anxiety, we'll focus on two: your third eye and your heart. In some ancient spiritual practices, the third eye—located in the space between your eyebrows—is regarded as the entryway to higher consciousness and knowledge, while your heart is the entryway to unconditional love and healing.

OPENING YOUR THIRD EYE

One of the definitions of *chakra* is "wheel of spinning energy." Thinking about this image helps when working with your third eye. When your third eye chakra is open (spinning) you are likely to be able to focus and concentrate better. However, when it is closed (not moving) you may become fearful of the unknown, be insecure, and have trouble processing your emotions. A blocked third eye can also connect to physical symptoms such as headaches and light sensitivity.

Your third eye is also said to impact your pineal gland, which is located deep within the center of your brain. This gland has a bearing on hormonal function and is responsible for producing melatonin, which can impact your waking and sleep rhythms—so a block in your third eye chakra might be the issue if you are having trouble sleeping. The pineal gland (as well as your hypothalamus) also influences your ability to regulate emotions.

Another way you know your third eye might be blocked or sluggish is if you often hear yourself asking people, "Are you mad at me?" If this is you, it is likely you are sensitive to shifts in energy, as people with anxiety often are. It is difficult to experience (let alone activate) joy when you are tuning in to non-movement of not only your own but someone else's emotions. Sound exhausting? Yes, it is. You feel things deeply but not in a way that is serving you.

The reason you pick up on fear, anxiety, or trauma is because it remains unhealed within you. It isn't until you digest the related emotions (by moving through the C.L.E.A.N.S.E.) that you can fully put your attention on joy. Your ingrained response is likely a way you learned to cope and manage the emotional shifts in others (probably during childhood) and hence the reason why balancing your chakras is also important when it comes to releasing ingrained responses. In addition to utilizing the C.L.E.A.N.S.E. method, here are some ways to keep your third eye balanced:

- Wear or diffuse essential oils (preferably nonsynthetic blends). Frankincense or sandalwood can help open the third eye.

- Tap on your third eye. Using your two peace-sign fingers, lightly tap between your eyebrows while breathing for thirty seconds.

- Meditate on or visualize the color indigo.

- Bring indigo foods (like blackberries and eggplant), colors, and scents (e.g., blueberry pie) into your life.

- Place your finger between your eyebrows and hum.

Now that your third eye is opening, move to your heart.

OPENING YOUR HEART

As mentioned earlier, people with anxiety often focus on the non-movement of others' emotions. Let's say you pick up on someone's resistance to expressing their feelings and connecting with you. You might think *What is wrong? What did I do?* Then you feel frustrated: *Don't they see how much I care? They don't appreciate anything I do.* This story starts to fuel your inner fire and an emotion does move, but it's anger. This does you no good because your mind is off and running with negative stories and responses. Chances are, you picked up on something that had nothing to do with you, but because you were feeling defensive your heart was probably blocked and you couldn't process your emotions.

I can recognize a blocked heart from a mile away. When this energy center is sluggish, emotions such as anger, frustration, or fear have a difficult time transforming into something new. Reactivity is one of the key indicators of a sluggish heart. With practice, you can learn to spot this and other signs of a heart center that would benefit from a little opening (which we talk about later).

Signs of a Sluggish Heart

- Blaming, pointing fingers
- Cold demeanor or inability to express affection
- Defensiveness
- Heavy fatigue
- Irritability
- Being resentful or stuck in anger

Here is the cool thing about your heart center. It has been shown to be far more powerful magnetically than the energy around your brain. Consider your heart to be a purifier—it cleanses the atmosphere both within you and outside of you. When it's in balance, your heart chakra helps you to notice and connect with joy—the flip side of anxiety.

One of the best ways to open your heart is to put your attention on nature. Nature is neutral yet invigorating—a place where joy can be infinite.

VISUALIZE...	WHICH REPRESENTS...
A beautiful tree	Strength, flexibility, stability
Ocean waves	Movement, transformation, tranquility
A meadow	Peace, serenity, stillness
A river	Purification, collaboration
Sunlight	Feeling healed, nurtured, reassured, supported
Doves	Connection, love, admiration
Moonlight	Transformation, health, empowerment

JOY IS A PURIFIER!

As you set your attention on joy, its energetic frequency is capable of cleansing and breaking old patterns. Think of joy as a way to clean your palate so you can get a pure taste of life. Each time you attune your third eye and heart center to joy, you are choosing to erase reactive patterns and bring forth your raw emotions. When you strip or block joy from your life, you are left with nothing but pure resistance.

It's important to note that happiness and joy aren't the same thing. Here is how to distinguish between the two to help you identify and activate joy specifically:

HAPPINESS	JOY
Is a temporary emotion	Is an infinite connection
Etches a moment in time	Erases reactive patterns
Involves experiencing good fortune	Involves experiencing the divine
Is more of an external experience	Is more of an internal experience
Can be conditional	Is unconditional
Can be altered	Is permanent
Is gleeful	Is peaceful, calming
Ignites	Cleanses
Is a burst of positive energy	Is resiliency

BELIEVE IN YOUR OWN ENERGY

I have had my fair share of clients who struggle with anxiety as they transition from adolescence into adulthood, wanting to be independent yet feeling so vulnerable and dependent. Middle-aged adults have also found their way to the C.L.E.A.N.S.E. method, sometimes after experiencing a tough event such as a medical diagnosis, divorce, or job loss. No matter who comes to me for help, I know part of my job is to support them in the process of believing in their energy.

Here is the thing: To wholly believe in your emotions and the energy they have to offer, you have to feel them. You can't think your way into this. After you hum (see C.L.E.A.N.S.E. Step 3: Emit), it becomes easier to activate your ability to focus on higher emotions such as joy. The hum gives you the energy to open up your third eye and heart center and zoom in on the thing that you know can bring you peace. Once you can visualize it, you will feel it in your heart. This is how activation works.

As you digest the energy of what you see, your tendency to over-process (thinking, ruminating) begins to loosen and is replaced by the feeling of belief and trust in the process of digesting your emotions. It's important to remember, though, that you could have it all—success, career, family, freedom—and still not feel anything; then it is likely that all your "success" will come at a cost. Anxiety is one of the main prices you will pay.

Sure, you could climb the corporate ladder or otherwise hustle and make a lot of money. However, when you get to the top, you may find yourself feeling overwhelmed by trying to keep it all in check. You may even feel a little paranoid, wonder if you can trust the people around you (are their intentions pure and good? does that person love you for the right reasons?), and ask yourself if this is what life is really all about. These are the kinds of thoughts people have when they don't take the time to digest their emotions along the way.

Let's take a moment here to walk through the C.L.E.A.N.S.E. steps discussed thus far.

TAKING STEPS

Let's say you find yourself hyperfocusing on an upcoming event you are planning such as a wedding, graduation, or dinner party. Here's how to follow C.L.E.A.N.S.E. in that situation.

Step 1: Clear Reactivity

- Tone vagus nerve (three presses, cat/cow stretch).

Step 2: Look Inward

- State the following stem sentences aloud to yourself, following each with your breath. Remember that your breath is the answer.
- How I feel in my body right now is _____ (Answer with your breath: *inhale...exhale...*). (Repeat three times.)
- Preparing for this party makes me feel _____ (*inhale...exhale...*). (Repeat two times.)
- And when I don't feel prepared it makes me feel _____ (*inhale...exhale...*). (Repeat two times.)

Step 3: Emit

- Hum three times.

Step 4: Activate Joy

- Visualize images in nature that symbolize feeling carefree, calm, and confident.

DIVINE TIME

When it comes to healing, there is human time and divine time. Human time is generally run by the ego—the part of you that wants to be quick, hurry up, and get things over with. Divine time, on the other hand, operates from the belief that everything happens in your life at the right moment—it *prepares* you, while human time *pushes* you.

When it comes to an emotional detox, you are on divine time whether you know it or not. It is not unusual for people who accept divine time to heal faster because they skip all the pointing fingers, blaming, fixing, rehashing, fleeing, and labeling. When you are on divine time, you go right to feeling. Here are the differences between human and divine time:

HUMAN TIME	DIVINE TIME
Sees an age	Is ageless
Wants to heal, get better	Is in the process of healing
Dismisses human connection	Honors human connection
Is fault-focused	Is feedback-focused
Thinks, measures	Feels, senses
Questions	Trusts
Operates on fear	Operates on faith

Whatever is happening in your life right now is because the universe, God, and/or your creator loves you so much and brought forth the exact situation that will provide you with the energy required to unite with your divine self or soul. Should you choose to feel what is happening (and it *is* a choice) and digest the emotions around it, you will gain exactly what you need to create your desires. As tough as it may be, and boy do I get that, your struggles with anxiety are what it took for you to wake up and feel.

Looking back now, I realize that I had to write six books and go through the process of healing after my husband's affair to produce the emotional detox mindset. Today, I live on divine time. This means staying focused on feeling (not thinking about) emotions. Sure, your mind will attempt to get you off track and old thoughts will resurface. When that happens, revisit the C.L.E.A.N.S.E., because transformation and freedom from anxiety come after you move through the formula.

RECAP

- Joy is a state of expansion.

- Activating joy means visualizing what you want to feel instead of your pain or hurt.

- Chakras that are out of balance impact your physical and mental well-being.

- Emotional detoxes run on divine time rather than human time.

- The universe brought certain situations, events, and people to support your growth and evolution.

CULTIVATE CALM

On the other side of anxiety is joy.

C.L.E.A.N.S.E. STEP 5
NOURISH

When you Nourish, you experience visualizations via all your senses. This continues to detox anxiety by downloading the higher-frequency energies you imagine into your physical and emotional body.

To *nourish* means to "cherish, foster, build up, or keep alive." During an emotional detox, you are nourishing your physical body and your spiritual body. This spiritual food, in the form of emotional energy, flows into your life, strengthening your relationships with yourself and with others.

Step 5 has a wonderful way of teaching you how to relax and soak up your creative potential. Just as you might take some of the principles of a yoga practice (like meditation or breathing) or a twelve-step program (like "Let go and let God") into your daily life, you can integrate your C.L.E.A.N.S.E. practice as well. You will learn how interacting with others from a state of processing (rather than reacting to) your emotions nourishes growth and healing in all areas of your life. You will also gain skills such as setting boundaries as a way to support and sustain joy.

This chapter is divided into two parts. First we'll go over exactly what Step 5 entails. Then we'll build your skills for increasing connection, enhancing communication, and setting healthy boundaries, all of which nourish us in so many ways.

VISUALIZING TO FEEL AND CONNECT

There is something important I want you to know about Step 5. What I have learned from teaching this method is that the tool of visualization can be misused, particularly by people with anxiety. If you are someone who uses visualization as a means to avoid or escape what you are feeling rather than connect to it, then you are going to find it hard to come back into your body after drifting into fantasy. No worries—this is the point of Step 5. You learn to appreciate (feel) your visualization so that by the time you get to the final step in the formula (Ease) you have embodied it.

Think about it—if you were to really assimilate a visualization of joy, love, and peace, then coming back into your body should feel great, right? I would imagine having these higher vibrations would feel gentle, light, and airy. If that's not your experience, then perhaps a part of you resisted the process. This may be because you either have learned to escape what you are feeling through visualization or you don't yet trust what you feel. Either way, with practice the C.L.E.A.N.S.E. will support your development.

In addition, if you are a great giver—meaning you have no problem giving time, attention, and energy (perhaps to the point of mental exhaustion) to others—Step 5 will teach you the benefits of supporting friends and family from a full rather than a depleted energy bank. As your vibration goes up, others will feel it—the more relaxed you become, the calmer others around you will seem. This is because they are experiencing the safety and security that your calmness brings.

Let's walk through a C.L.E.A.N.S.E. to this point.

TAKING STEPS

Step 1: Clear Reactivity

- Three acupressure presses, neck stretches.

Step 2: Look Inward

- How I feel in my body right now is _____ (*inhale... exhale...*). *Remember: Do not answer; your breath is the answer.*

Step 3: Emit

- Hum three times.

Step 4: Activate Joy

- See it! Visualize healthy, calm, loving communication. Consider looking to nature; for example, to see how birds communicate with one another or how a cat feeds her kittens.

Step 5: Nourish

- Feel it! Allow yourself to experience these visualizations through feeling. Hear the cat purring, imagine the soft fur, and so on. Observe, appreciate, and allow inner movement to take place in your body. Notice how your breathing elongates or deepens from the process. Notice how relaxation increases. This is the kind of state from which you will learn how to communicate and connect.

PROMOTING RELAXATION

If you have ever had a conversation with a tense or stressed-out person, you know how difficult and anxiety-provoking that can be. Being in these states is when you are most likely to resort to old ways of coping and reacting as conscious and unconscious ways of protecting yourself. It is through reactions (such as defensiveness) that your body believes it is resisting an attack. In this state, there is no possible way to process your emotions.

For someone with anxiety, having someone raise their voice or give them a dirty look can feel like just such an attack. Whether it was abusive or not, it feels that way to the person who is in high levels of reactivity. On the other hand, if you are the one slamming the door or yelling, you probably experience a huge drop in energy. Learning how to both speak and listen from a relaxed state is key to living a life with more joy and ease.

If you tend to want to be right and/or you tend to focus on how you have been wronged, then this mindset can contribute to resisting the opportunity to learn or to polish your communication skills. I always ask my clients, "Do you want to be right or relaxed?" Since most of them come to me for anxiety, they want nothing more than to experience some peace of mind.

Let's take a moment now and C.L.E.A.N.S.E. how an attachment to being right may be showing up for you.

TAKING STEPS

Step 1: Clear Reactivity

- Three acupressure presses, neck stretch, cat/cow seated stretch.

Step 2: Look Inward

- How I feel in my body right now is _____ (*inhale... exhale...*).
- Being right makes me feel _____ (*inhale...exhale...*).
- Being wrong makes me feel _____ (*inhale... exhale...*).
- Blaming others makes me feel _____ (*inhale... exhale...*).
- Blaming myself makes me feel _____ (*inhale... exhale...*).

Step 3: Emit

- Hum three times (inhale between hums—take a moment and notice the inhalation naturally rising in you).

Step 4: Activate Joy

- Visualize an image in nature that represents pride, worthiness, and security, such as a tall sunflower.

Step 5: Nourish

- Feel that tall sunflower standing proud. Inhale and receive the energy of this feeling. Integrate this feeling into your body!

Pause for a moment and notice your body after moving through the formula. Notice your inhale and exhale. Notice if your body is looking to move more freely; perhaps your neck and shoulders are looking to move around. If so, let them! Move and breathe freely; this is a sign that you are absorbing nourishing energy!

LEARNING HOW TO CONNECT WITH OTHERS

Now that you are more relaxed and settled in your body, we can talk some more about connection. Connection is a basic need. While it is normal and healthy to move in and out of states of disconnection periodically, remaining in a disconnected state can take its toll on even the most loving relationships. If you are someone with anxiety, it is likely you are sensitive to disconnection, meaning that when things between you and someone else are not right (tense, awkward), it can feel torturous. While someone less anxious might be able to shrug it off, you could be really affected by that. In some cases, this is where anxiety can develop into depression.

Practicing the C.L.E.A.N.S.E. method on a regular (daily) basis will help build up your stamina so you aren't so sensitive to others' opinions, moods, or anxiety for that matter. In addition, understanding what your role is when things are "off" between you and another will help. Maintaining healthy connections in your world is made easier when you express appreciation to others and when you listen deeply; tips for how to do both are discussed later in this chapter.

CONTRIBUTING TO THE SPACE

While it may seem the best solution for awkward, tense moments is to tell another person to get their act together, as you probably know, learning how to communicate in a kinder, gentler way is a better choice. You don't get to peace by focusing on wanting, asking, or waiting for others to change. After all, those are ways you react to (rather than feel and digest) your emotions of frustration, hurt, anger, and feeling overwhelmed.

What you *can* do, however, is help foster the space that exists between you and another where you exchange words and interactions. If you are not sure what I am talking about, imagine sitting across from someone or standing a few feet away, facing each other. The space in between is where connection and disconnection can occur. If you fill the space with reactivity, you are likely to exchange triggers and reactivity. (Each time you move through the C.L.E.A.N.S.E., you are in fact choosing not only to heal but also to contribute to your personal space in a beneficial way.) On the other hand, when you allow yourself to process your emotions, you become a source of energy by being you, and the space becomes free from reactivity.

While it may seem like you have a lot of work ahead of you, the more you C.L.E.A.N.S.E., the more readily you'll create an atmosphere for healthy exchanges. I used to take tough discussions or heated exchanges really hard. Now, rather than go off on my own and ruminate, I go through the steps of the C.L.E.A.N.S.E. After all, I know I wouldn't be so triggered if there were not something coming up in me to be healed. With that in mind, let's progress through Steps 1, 2, 3, 4, and 5 one more time.

TAKING STEPS

Step 1: Clear Reactivity

- Three acupressure presses, neck stretch.

Step 2: Look Inward

- How I feel in my body right now is _____ (*inhale... exhale...*).

- Having that conversation made me feel _____ (*inhale...exhale...*).

- Hearing that tone of voice made me feel _____ (*inhale...exhale...*).

- Being in that situation made me feel _____ (*inhale... exhale...*).

Step 3: Emit

- Hum three times.

Step 4: Activate Joy

- Visualize an image in nature that represents safety, such as quiet sounds or a gentle breeze.

Step 5: Nourish

- Feel it! (soft breeze on your skin, gentle sounds in nature)

I have found that after you C.L.E.A.N.S.E., the conversation changes. What you were originally focused on shifts. If you were focused on being right, you may shift to focusing on being relaxed. From this calm space, you can open up dialogue.

FOSTERING APPRECIATION

Offering appreciation not only keeps the lines of communication open; it also creates an environment of safety. When people feel safe, they are more open to being flexible and listening to and understanding the opinions, comments, and concerns of another. If tension is high between you and someone else, then it is likely appreciations are low. Unlike gratitude, where you might express or feel thankful for what someone says or does, appreciation runs within similar frequencies as joy. While you might not see the difference between the two, if you tune in you might feel it. Here is a little snapshot of how these two responses are similar yet unique:

GRATITUDE	APPRECIATION
Comes from the Latin root *gratus*, meaning "pleasing or thankful." It's a feeling of thankfulness after receiving an act or gesture of kindness.	Is the recognition or enjoyment of the good qualities of someone or something.
Thank you for...	You made me feel...

You can see how gratitude tends to be more focused on an act or gesture (like when someone holds the door for you), while appreciation tends to focus on the qualities (like how someone makes you feel when they hold the door for you). One is not better than the other—in fact, you could even blend the two. Give it a try. See how it *feels*.

Begin by reading this stem sentence aloud, completing it for yourself as you pay attention to your inhale and exhale:

Thank you for _____ (*inhale...exhale...*).

Read this stem sentence aloud, completing it for yourself as you pay attention to your inhale and exhale:

It made me feel _____ (*inhale...exhale...*).

Which one gave you more inner movement and how did you know? If you have anxiety, it is likely the second one made you feel uncomfortable, maybe even a little tight in your chest. Keep in mind that tightness is a sensation. You may be accustomed to seeing tension as a sign that anxiety is getting worse; however, at this point in the C.L.E.A.N.S.E. method (after the hum) if you are observing some tightness (in the absence of chronic thinking), then you are processing your emotions!

As corny as it may seem to hear yourself speak that way aloud, know that the movement you receive inside means you are growing and strengthening your skills. Now let's blend gratitude and appreciation together. It will look something like this:

- I really appreciated it when you asked me if I needed anything (the act of kindness)—it made me feel (the appreciation) fortunate and blessed.

- I really appreciated it when you returned my call (action or gesture)—it made me feel (the appreciation) hopeful about this opportunity.

- I really appreciated it when you apologized the other day (act of kindness)—it made me feel (the appreciation) loved.

Introducing new ways of speaking and responding may take you out of your comfort zone. Consider practicing aloud on yourself first before trying it on another person. You may even write out the sentences on paper if talking aloud is too intimidating. In any case, keep practicing and don't rush—remember that you are on divine time.

DEEP LISTENING

Up until this point in the C.L.E.A.N.S.E. you have been encouraged to tune in, to listen to your breath and bodily feedback or sensations. As you take your Nourish step, you are encouraged to renew your ability to listen, *truly* listen to others. While you may be the one who has not felt heard, validated, or appreciated, I assure you that moving through the C.L.E.A.N.S.E. regularly will soften these triggers.

If you have been battling or managing anxiety, it is likely that your listening skills have become rusty. When you are dealing with medium to high levels of anxiety, interacting with others can seem like a chore. Reintroducing yourself to the power of listening while on this journey will be well worth it.

To truly listen to another human being, you have to be okay with pausing, sensing, and feeling the present moment. If you are someone who is always running, keeping yourself distracted, or never really letting your guard down, then it would make sense that listening to another human being might seem rather complicated. What you may not realize yet is that listening to another person not only nourishes your relationships and partnerships, but also puts you in an internal state of processing your emotions!

Yes, when you truly listen to another, you have to be in a state of processing. Remember, the essential ingredients for processing emotions are oxygen, awareness, observation (of self and others), and free will (your choice to listen). On the other hand, when you listen from a state of reactivity, you are more likely to interrupt, defend, get distracted, or think about what you will say in return. By now, you understand that these were ways that you were repressing the emotions that were coming up to be healed. So essentially you were revisiting old patterns. No wonder your relationships were feeling compromised!

In addition to your C.L.E.A.N.S.E. practice, you can strengthen your listening skills by keeping the following in mind:

- Listening is a choice to pause and connect with your breath.
- Practice your ability to engage eye contact.

- Put all distractions (e.g., your phone) aside or on mute.

- Face the person you are listening to.

- Repeat what you hear: "What I hear you saying is..."

- Use the other person's words when you reply and avoid reinterpretation.

- Ask the person if there is anything they want to add before you end the conversation.

From here on, experience your choice to listen to another as a way to create mutual healing and connection.

SETTING BOUNDARIES

If you are having difficulty speaking up for yourself or expressing your needs, I assure you this will be covered in C.L.E.A.N.S.E. Step 6: Surrender. Before heading there, it is important you continue nourishing yourself by learning to set healthy boundaries. Many people with anxiety have a lot of confusion around this. If you have not set boundaries within yourself, it means up until now you have allowed your mind to bully your body. In other words, by using thinking as a way to cope, you pushed away feeling.

It may seem like setting boundaries would happen on a more physical level, kind of like drawing a line in the sand, but consider that these skills begin on an internal level. Each time you choose Step 1 (Clear Reactivity) and do those three acupressure presses slightly above your navel followed by neck stretches, you are in fact setting a boundary within yourself. You are saying, "Body, I hear you and I am choosing to heal." As you practice this technique, it will become easier for you to set external boundaries. Here are some ways this can occur:

- Rather than send back a reactive text, choose to pause, and give yourself the time and space before responding.

- Rather than become defensive, choose to heal what is showing up in you by C.L.E.A.N.S.E.ing.
- Say no or set limits because you recognize reactivity.
- Say no or set limits because it feels right in your gut or body.
- Prioritize feeling over reacting.

My hope is that you see how fostering connection and honoring the space between you and another and really listening provides a healthy foundation for establishing boundaries. Rather than boundaries becoming something you enforce, they will evolve organically into a way to support (rather than protect) the processing of your emotions.

RECAP

- In your daily C.L.E.A.N.S.E., the Nourish step encourages you to feel your visualizations. Make them come alive through your sense of smell, touch, sounds, etc.
- Outside of your daily C.L.E.A.N.S.E. ritual, the Nourish step provides you with the skills for strengthening connection with yourself and others.
- Build relationships by fostering gratitude and appreciation.
- Listening is a way to process emotions.
- Setting boundaries happens organically through your C.L.E.A.N.S.E. practice.

CULTIVATE CALM

Choosing to process your emotions as they are is no different from choosing to be you!

C.L.E.A.N.S.E. STEP 6
SURRENDER

When you Surrender, you allow a new way of being to manifest in your life. This continues to detox anxiety by freeing you from the need to control your emotions.

When it comes to spirituality and your emotions, surrender is never about giving up, giving in, or throwing in the towel. To surrender means to *allow*. Step 6 in the C.L.E.A.N.S.E. is about allowing that which you choose to create. In this step, you will ask yourself: *If I am not resisting and anxious, what qualities will I be allowing into my life? How will I know when I have absorbed them?*

What I love about the Surrender step is that it is direct. This is because it comes with some assertiveness. There is no wishy-washy behavior in this step. Unlike other times when you might have attempted to feel your emotions and ended up feeling bad, sappy, or like a pushover, the C.L.E.A.N.S.E. guides you to a place where you are able to speak your truth, and since it is *your* truth, why would you want it to be anything less than assertive? To get there, you'll practice allow statements—"I allow uncertainty…"; "I allow freedom…"; "I allow truth…"; "I allow forgiveness…"—that take your life in a more solid, positive, loving direction. This is because the C.L.E.A.N.S.E. works in accordance with the spiritual law of detachment.

THE SPIRITUAL LAW OF DETACHMENT

Anxiety happens when you give things too much meaning. You overfocus on the interpretation rather than experiencing the emotions submerged within the thoughts, words, and actions. To put it frankly, you put a lot of significance into other people's reactions. You made triggers count more than feelings—that is, until now. I encourage you to have faith that the previous five steps of the C.L.E.A.N.S.E. provide you with the energy you will need to create and make your allow statements. Your allow statements will help you become naturally aligned with the spiritual law of detachment.

The spiritual law of detachment (which is taught by author and spiritual teacher Deepak Chopra) states that to get anything in the physical world, you have to detach from the outcome or what the results may be. What the C.L.E.A.N.S.E. has shown me about this law is that when your emotions are in flow, they naturally place you in a state of nonattachment. This happens by directing you away from the end point (what you want or, in most cases, don't want), instead giving you the means to surrender and allow the vibration of higher consciousness to emerge.

When you reach this state of higher consciousness, don't be surprised if insights, words, or ideas come up in your mind. Rather than whisk them away, I encourage you to sit with them for a second or two, even play around with your breath as you shape your newfound energy into the physical via your "I allow" statement.

CREATING YOUR ALLOW STATEMENTS

There are two ways to create an allow statement:

1. The first is to state what feels natural and allow whatever is coming through you to express itself through your own words. Words like "freedom," "love," "peace," and "strength," are a few that may come to mind.

2. The second way to create an allow statement is to describe in a few words the *opposite* of how you have been reacting or coping. For example, if you cope with feeling frustrated by bickering with others, your "I allow" statement might be: "I allow harmony, I allow agreement, I allow connection."

After I'd guided Suzanne through the C.L.E.A.N.S.E. she realized (after her "I feel" statement and taking two breaths) that she still felt blocked and guarded. When I asked her how she coped with this feeling, she said she tried to fix things or run different scenarios and solutions through her mind. I pointed out that the opposite of fixing is breaking. While saying "I allow breaking" felt a little strange, she and I sat with it and came up with this allow statement: "I allow a breakthrough." This immediately felt right to her.

This is why I encourage you to let yourself sit with the process, because I am confident that within seconds your "I allow" statement will start to take shape. Keep in mind that you can never go wrong with allow statements; they command peace, transformation, confidence, and more. The important part is: How does it make you feel? Does it fit?

If you have not yet developed a practice using the C.L.E.A.N.S.E., know that this step will be easier once you do. Creating an "I allow" statement from a state of reactivity is a whole different experience than creating an "I allow" statement from digested emotions. Once you get the hang of it, you may even find the Surrender step to be fun and interesting. It is like opening a hidden vault to what your soul has been attempting to create all along.

To support you, I want to share a list of reacting/coping responses transformed into surrender (allow) statements. To be quite honest, it is not unusual for me to pull up Google on my phone and search for words to describe the opposite of how reactivity is showing up. More often than not, I am blown away at how reactivity covers up exactly what you need to develop in order to experience more joy in your life. This step allows you to claim your innermost desires, unleash what was previously holding you captive (reactivity), and more.

REACTING OR COPING	SURRENDERING (ALLOW STATEMENT)
Babbling	I allow quiet and solitude.
Checking	I allow looseness, I allow space.
Complaining	I allow acceptance.
Confusion	I allow communication, I allow clarity.
Crying	I allow laughter, I allow happiness.
Defending	I allow surrender, I allow letting go.
Escaping	I allow stillness.
Fighting	I allow peacemaking, I allow contentment, I allow calm.
Fixing	I allow breaking through, I allow breaking apart or shattering.
Giving in	I allow assertiveness, I allow expression.
Guarding	I allow openness, I allow trust, I allow vulnerability.
Judging	I allow approval, I allow freedom, I allow compassion.
Managing	I allow development, I allow skills.
Resisting	I allow movement, I allow healing, I allow transformation.
Ruminating	I allow carefree, I allow lighthearted, I allow peace.
Thinking	I allow feeling, I allow sensations.
Trying, pleasing	I allow discomfort, I allow presence, I allow pain, I allow dullness.
Withdrawing	I allow connection.
Worry	I allow growth, I allow faith.

Because the Surrender step comes on the heels of nourishment, your emotions are already processing and in a state of flow. This non-reactive state allows you to remain fairly neutral (untriggered) as you state these commands aloud to yourself. Without practicing the five preceding steps, you are likely to resist, as you may imagine something being taken away from you (like protection or power).

As you practice the C.L.E.A.N.S.E., this tendency to focus on fear of loss will dissipate, and as this occurs, your "I allow" statements will become stronger. In other words, you will be able to *allow* something into your process, even if it is uncomfortable, because you are confident that it is related to you gaining full energy. It doesn't have to be perfect in order for you to benefit.

COMMAND IT!

Neville Goddard—a profound teacher and author—wrote in his 1944 book *Feeling Is the Secret*, "Your feelings create the pattern from which your world is fashioned, and a change of feeling is a change of pattern." The challenge is that what most of us have been calling an emotion is a reaction. In other words, you can't change a feeling through thinking, demanding, or explaining. Those are reactions. This is why the C.L.E.A.N.S.E. is so revolutionary; it clears patterns by promoting (rather than interrupting) feeling states!

After you create your "I allow" statement, you will then make a command to the universe. However, don't confuse commanding with demanding. When you demand something, it often comes from a place of reactivity. For example, you might demand that your kids clean their rooms or demand that a business give you your money back. Demands often happen from desperate, frustrated states. Commands, on the other hand, come from a place of already having energy. You don't see yourself as needing something per se, but rather you are choosing to go out on a limb and command it. A command comes from a place of feeling solid and firm in who you are and what you believe. Here are some additional ways you can tell the difference between demand and command:

DEMAND	COMMAND
Tainted by unworthiness	Feels worthy
A reaction	A decision
Fear driven	Faith driven
Rooted in feeling disrespected	Rooted in a place of having respect
Wants power and authority	Has power and authority
Stems from struggle	Stems from integrity
Feels forced	Flows

To be an effective commander, it is important that you learn how to use your voice. This is why I waited to discuss speaking (communicating with others) until now. In the Nourish step, you learned the benefits of listening and how to diffuse reactivity through appreciation. When it comes to your daily C.L.E.A.N.S.E., how you command the tone of your voice matters.

USING YOUR VOICE

As you become adept at practicing C.L.E.A.N.S.E., you will notice that there is quite a difference between speaking from reactivity (before C.L.E.A.N.S.E.) versus speaking from the neutral space of healing (after C.L.E.A.N.S.E.). The conversation changes. Not just in the words you choose and the pauses between them, but also in how you enunciate or neutralize your tone. What I have learned is that before C.L.E.A.N.S.E., dialogue typically sounds scattered, talkative, defensive, and apologetic. It is almost as if you feel bad about what you are saying. You want to express what is on your mind, but hesitate because you are not sure if it is a good idea. The Surrender step will help you.

As you state your allow statements aloud, you are beginning to develop an ability to use your voice in a powerful way. After all, isn't the fear of losing power how you got in this position in the first place? Following are some guidelines for strengthening your speaking voice without squashing your emotions. After reading each one, incorporate these guidelines into the allow statements that follow.

Strengthening Your Voice Without Squashing Emotions

- **Breathe between each allow statement.** Remember, one breath is an inhale and an exhale. Be mindful of not short-circuiting your breath. When you short-circuit your breath (meaning you exhale quickly or overfocus on your inhale), the breath never gets a chance to get into the lower lobes of your lungs as well as your lower chakras (energy centers), where you can gain a sense of grounding and centeredness.

- **Speak from your gut.** You will notice that when you have a premature exhale and you are not rooted into the lower half of your body (pelvic floor, hips, legs), this impacts the sound of your voice. You want to feel like you are speaking from your core, as this will likely lower the tone of your voice.

- **Make it a statement.** When you state your allow statement, be sure you end the statement as a command and not a question. As a question your voice is likely to go up at the end. You are looking to create a solid tone that stays even all the way through your statement.

- **Direct your gaze.** When making your allow statement, direct your gaze on a set point so your eyes are not wandering around the room.

Next, apply these guidelines to the following allow statements. Practice each one aloud. After you state all three, sit for a moment and observe your breathing.

1. I allow ease.

2. I allow enthusiasm.

3. I allow willingness.

Let's take a moment now to review the daily C.L.E.A.N.S.E. steps that we have discussed so far.

TAKING STEPS

Step 1: Clear Reactivity

- Tone vagus nerve with three acupressure presses, cat/cow stretch; choose to heal.

Step 2: Look Inward

- How I feel in my body right now is _____ (*inhale... exhale...*).

Step 3: Emit

- Hum three times, rinsing all those coping and defense mechanisms.

Step 4: Activate Joy

- See it! Visualize what you are choosing to create in nature.

Step 5: Nourish

- Feel it! Experience the sensations of what you are creating or seeing in your body.

Step 6: Surrender

- Command it! Create and state your allow statements.

EMBRACING THE LAW OF LEAST RESISTANCE

Author and spiritual teacher Deepak Chopra often refers to the law of least resistance as the law of least effort. This principle reminds you to accept your present situation as is, to resist the temptation to change or cope with what may or may not be happening in your life. Keep in mind that during the emotional detox journey it is common to discover that how you have been coping is by resisting exactly what you need to move forward and have the life you desire!

For example, if you are someone who wants to lose weight and perhaps you cope with feeling bloated or heavy by telling yourself *I am sick and tired of feeling this way* or *I don't want to feel this way in my clothes anymore*, you may react by overfocusing on a diet or putting a lot of pressure on yourself to stop eating certain things. This requires a lot of resistance and persistence on your part.

There is an old saying: "What you resist persists." If you resist feeling, non-movement will persist in your body. Using this example, what you may really need is to be kinder, gentler, and more patient with yourself. It isn't until you cleanse these coping mechanisms that you will be able to create the changes you would like to make in a more productive way.

When it comes to the Surrender step, your command is not about being better; it is about cleansing your need to cope with, manage, and control your feelings. As awareness increases, you will be blown away by what you notice and by the ways you consciously and unconsciously coped. Mechanisms such as clinging to another person or overwhelming yourself with work may have been ways you resisted experiencing the emotions that were attempting to move inside you. You can be free now. Your allow statement will guide you in the right direction.

HOW TO RECOGNIZE WHEN YOU'RE PROCESSING EMOTIONS

After you state two or three allow statements, pause for a moment and notice your body. Observe your inhale and exhale. Notice if you are able to observe yourself with nonjudgment. It is not unusual for you to feel buzzing, tingly sensations at this point (and even before this point) in the formula. Consider these sensations to be feedback that you are receiving the energy from your processed emotions. Following are some signs to look for. Your job at this point is to observe without effort.

Signs of Receiving Energy from Processing Emotions

- Feeling more neutral
- Bodily movement (e.g., you might be moving your shoulders and neck around without thinking about it)
- Space between thoughts
- Increased saliva in mouth
- Natural breathing
- Tingling
- Buzzing feeling
- Detachment from outcome

This feedback from your body is valuable, and similar to the way you would be careful when carrying something valuable and precious, be mindful to not disturb the processing of your emotions.

DISCOVERING YOUR PURPOSE

Don't be surprised if Step 6 opens the doorway to you discovering your soul's purpose. I believe that we are all meant to feel our emotions so that we can contribute and discover joy. With that said, you might also unearth other things such as how your soul wants to express, expand, and contribute to the planet.

I had a client who was experiencing high levels of anxiety due to the debt she owed a friend for covering her rent for two years. She tried everything—network marketing, a small startup business, hiring coaches, taking on extra jobs—but no matter what, she seemed to remain stuck. So I asked, "How do you cope with this anxiety?" She told me she worried, tried harder, put herself down, and became obsessed with not having enough money. Together we moved through the steps of the C.L.E.A.N.S.E. After rinsing away all those coping mechanisms, by the time we got to surrender, some of her statements sounded like this:

- I allow praise.
- I allow dignity.
- I allow worthy.
- I allow powerful.
- I allow choice.
- I allow freedom.

Once she stated those statements aloud and completed the final step of the formula, some new, wiser information came forward. I said to her, "Hey, rather than seeing all these efforts as trying to get you more money, perhaps your desire to pay coaches and work side jobs is something you enjoy. Perhaps your soul desires exploring ways to create money." As soon as I framed it that way, I saw relief on her face. "Yes, I do enjoy trying many things," she said. "The way you framed it feels so much better, lighter, and freer." From that point on, she was able to accept and embrace herself for who she was. She no longer viewed these tactics as trying to make money but rather as being and allowing herself to create financial flow. This shift gave her the energy to feel secure and at ease about her choices. Interestingly enough, it also got her to slow down and focus more on one or two things rather than scatter her ideas.

Here is the thing: Anxiety never wanted you to be different; it wanted you to be you. As you allow yourself to experience your emotions, you get to rinse your need to cope. This is how the laws of detachment and least resistance work. You can't tell yourself to let it go, move on, focus on something else. This will only make things seem impossible. As you purify the ways in which you have been confusing feeling with coping, the real you will come forward as you integrate your soul fully into your body.

RECAP

- Surrender is not about giving up; it is about allowing.

- You can create your allow statements in two ways: (1) state what feels natural and (2) describe the *opposite* of how you have been reacting or coping.

- Command what your soul desires by developing your speaking voice.

- Surrender is in alignment with the law of detachment and least resistance.

- Know the signs of processing.

- Uncovering resistance may lead to discovering your purpose!

CULTIVATE CALM

Anxiety taught you how to hold on; now your emotions will teach you how to be free.

C.L.E.A.N.S.E. STEP 7
EASE

When you step into Ease, you make an "I am" statement that completes the daily anxiety detox by harmonizing mind, body, and spirit.

As you move into the final step, know that this is not about living a life without challenge or stress. That is simply unrealistic. To live in ease means knowing that everything that is occurring in your life has purpose. While you may have been inclined to prevent, stop, or protect yourself from certain experiences, your soul is hungry for them; you just might not have realized it yet. If you believe that your life is a hot mess, think again—you are on the verge of a breakthrough. I have seen it so many times: People arrive to their session in tears, fearful that everything is beyond repair— that is, until they experience the magic of the C.L.E.A.N.S.E.

What this final Ease step has taught me is that there is no "perfect," and by excluding certain experiences you may be caught in the web of perfection. For example, you may be so worried about saying the wrong thing or acting the wrong way that you deny certain experiences and forget that even experiences that carry a thread of disappointment or rejection can present opportunities for growth. While you may think, *Who the heck wants rejection?*, might I remind you that it is not the feeling of rejection that is the problem, but rather your reaction to it. In the end, it is all energy; however, you can only experience it when that energy (in the form of your emotions) is in motion.

CONNECTING TO YOUR "I AM" PRESENCE

Ease connects you to your "I am" presence. While this may not seem like a big deal, when it comes to people with anxiety I find that they have hindered their "I am." Rather than stepping into their magnificence, they misuse this incredible phrase by thinking or saying things like "I am so worried" or "I am such a basket case" or "I know I am difficult sometimes." Your "I am" is sacred; just writing these negative statements makes me feel so sad!

Here is the thing: Your "I am" is always with you. Each time you inhale and exhale, you enter the "I am" space. This space can only be experienced through presence. Because you have worked so hard at controlling your feelings, the sensation of the "I am" presence may be dull, but I assure you it is not gone. No worries; each time you C.L.E.A.N.S.E. your body recalls the memory of your "I am" presence.

Think of the Ease step as merging your "I am" with the joy frequency:

I am (state of processing your emotions) + joy (state of expansion) = oneness

Being in a state of oneness builds a platform of confidence, faith, and trust—not just trust with others, but also within yourself.

This chapter walks you through this process. It begins by converting your "I allow" statement or Surrender, reconstructing what it means to need, and diving into oneness and learning to value and recognize the "I am" in others. In the end, you will learn to trust what you feel rather than distance yourself from it. This allows you to spend less time being your anxious self and more time being your true self. Let's begin by standing tall.

STANDING TALL

Take a moment now and stand up tall. Have your two feet side by side. If you can't stand, then sit up as best you can; if necessary, put a stool under your feet. I always say that to be fully present in your "I am" you want to make a connection with Mother Earth. So, if you are sitting down I encourage you to get up for a minute, with your chin parallel to the floor, shoulders back and down, because your "I am" is a feeling of expansion.

Let's begin at the top of the formula. In this example we will C.L.E.A.N.S.E. a coping mechanism I see time and time again with anxious clients: the habit of letting others off the hook. This means you expect little from others; you see them as weak or incapable of meeting your needs. So rather than holding others accountable for their actions, you have learned to cope by either distancing yourself or putting more responsibilities on yourself. (Whether you can relate to this cycle or not, I guarantee that you know someone who can, and as you develop your C.L.E.A.N.S.E.ing abilities, it won't matter so much who it is for—we are all one. Therefore, as you process you become a powerful influence on this planet.)

Here is an example of how this final Ease step works as the culmination of the C.L.E.A.N.S.E. process:

TAKING STEPS

Step 1: Clear Reactivity

- Three acupressure presses, neck stretch, seated stretch, gaze toward floor.

Step 2: Look Inward

- How I feel in my body right now is _____ (*inhale... exhale...*).

- Being in my body right now is _____ (*inhale... exhale...*).

- Being still makes me feel _____ (*inhale...exhale...*).

- Ignoring my feelings makes me feel _____ (*inhale... exhale...*).

- Paying attention to my feelings makes me feel _____ (*inhale...exhale...*).

Step 3: Emit

- Hum three times (inhale, exhale into the hum while closing your mouth).

Step 4: Activate Joy

- See it! Visualize being present and complete in nature.

Step 5: Nourish

- Feel it! Imagine the sensations of wholeness, nothing missing.

Step 6: Surrender

- "I allow" statement: *I allow presence, I allow completion, I allow wholeness...*

Step 7: Ease

- "I am" statement: *I am presence, I am completion, I am wholeness...*

RECEIVING ENERGY

Your "I am" presence is a continuous state of receiving energy. Rather than being afraid or ambivalent about experiencing your emotions, instead you embrace them as a resource for uplifting yourself. When your emotions are fully digested and processed in your body, you elevate your awareness. This increases your resiliency and ability to see your situation from an expanded viewpoint. To train yourself in receiving rather than depleting energy, I suggest giving yourself a chance to marinate in the "I am" energy by stating your "I am" statements aloud then letting this energy be absorbed into your body.

Think of it like this: Imagine you got a nail in your car's tire and for the last few weeks you have been nervous about it going flat. You take it to the car repair shop fully expecting you are going to have to pay for a new tire; instead you find out that you can patch the tire for $25. You feel relieved and lucky; perhaps this is a sign that things are moving in a better direction.

Now, let's look at this from the emotional detox perspective. The tire was an opportunity for you to C.L.E.A.N.S.E. your fear of immobility, being strapped down, feeling limited or stuck in your current situation. The universe loves you so much that it sent you this opportunity in a kind and gentle way. When you live in your "I am" presence, you are more likely to witness these mini miracles all around you. To do so, it will be important for you to practice learning how to let energy land in your body. Here are some tips for doing this and basking in the "I am":

- Embrace pauses.

- Feel before you speak.

- Exhale through your nose rather than your mouth.

- Focus on the lower half of your body (hips, legs, feet) on exhale. This helps you connect to the feeling of stability, safety, and security.

- Close your eyes after stating your "I am."

- Place your hand on your heart when stating your "I am."
- Give yourself thirty seconds to absorb your "I am" before moving on.

THE LAW OF VIBRATION

According to the law of vibration taught by author and motivational speaker Bob Proctor, everything moves and nothing rests. When you get stuck in fear or worry or compare yourself to others, you are resisting movement. Anxiety is an unconscious attempt to hold vibration still, manage it through thinking, labels, and reactions. Living with ease means learning to let love in.

As you move into the "I am" space, you will learn to let go of this resistance. Being in a state of resistance means that you have to push away or put an internal wall up to resist feeling. This is exhausting and causes you to unnecessarily waste and give away energy. Living in your "I am" presence means learning to live in accordance with the law of vibration, a law that essentially means that nothing in life is permanent because everything is constantly changing. Inside you will choose to embrace the ebbs and flows of life. The bottom line is that we will all go through periods of instability. This is how this law works; everything is always in motion and always changing.

Keep in mind that the C.L.E.A.N.S.E. method is twofold:

1. It allows you to rinse toxicity (reactivity) from your life (letting go).
2. It is the formula for manifesting joy!

Notice how the formula changes the idea of letting go, from a fear-based place into a love-based, "I am" presence.

LETTING GO (I CHOOSE...)	LETTING LOVE IN (I AM...)
Releasing	Receiving
Nonresistance	Marinating
Observing	Being
Flowing	Embracing

This final step (Ease) prepares you for this transition.

RECONSTRUCTING NEEDS INTO DESIRES

The word "need" has two definitions:

1. To be important, essential

2. Necessity, obligation

I have learned that many people with anxiety see needs as weaknesses. In other words, to need something or someone means you are a burden. This could not be further from the truth. In the emotional detox journey, needs are obligations. Your "I am" presence is your soul obligation.

I believe your soul made a commitment to experience life on this planet. There is something your soul desired. Your "I am" presence allows you to connect with those inner desires to remember what your soul was looking to experience. In the emotional detox mindset, needs are desires.

Sure, as a physical being, you need food, water, and shelter. However, to fulfill your innermost desires you also need connection, physical touch, love, a sense of belonging, and purpose. Whether you choose to focus on the physical, the spiritual, or both, the bottom line is that you need energy. Moving into your "I am" means you will see your emotions as spiritual food and nourishment for your soul.

The way I see it, you would not desire balance, calm, freedom, and peace if it weren't already in you. Your job is not to get or find ease; it is to learn how to be aware of how ease already exists. Your desires will take you there. I suggest noticing what you are interested in or drawn to without judgment. Here are some ways this process of noticing shows up in your life:

- A thought keeps coming back without charge. This means that you revisit an idea without being attached to it. For example, you might be drawn to getting your real estate license or taking a cooking class.

- You feel a natural pull toward a new direction. Perhaps you are looking to visit somewhere new, check out a new store, or connect with an old friend. Listen.

- You have thoughts or moments when you would like to forgive. Maybe there is someone in your life who hurt you, and while there is still a sting of the past, there is a stronger part of you that wants to invest in your future.

- You find yourself interested in developing hobbies or picking up something you once enjoyed as a child; for example, singing, playing an instrument, riding a bike, painting, writing, etc.

These are examples of your soul speaking to you. It is telling you where and how you can gain the energy you need to serve your obligations on this planet.

APPLYING THE PAUSE PRACTICE TO ANXIETY

Once you learn to move into your "I am," you will gradually gain respect for this sacred space. You will know this because you won't want to disrupt it. Just as how you might leave the lid on top of a pot of rice while it is cooking (so the rice can fully absorb the water), you will treat your "I am" space in the same way. This is along the lines of marinating; however, realistically, you will get interrupted. Developing your pause statements will allow you to continue to stay connected to the "I am" energy.

Pause statements are phrases you use to give yourself time to feel rather than think or react quickly. If people (colleagues, friends, children) expect you to answer them instantly you might want some pause statements handy that will give you time to digest your emotions. Here are a few:

- Let me sit with that.
- I need a moment to digest your question.
- Give me a moment to digest before I answer you.
- I am feeling this out; I will get back to you.
- Let me take a breath and I will let you know.

Some other examples specific to someone experiencing anxiety include:

- I am feeling a little sped up; let me take a second and reset myself.
- My body is telling me I need a little breather.
- I am feeling a little distracted, so I'll stretch my legs before we continue.

The cool part is, when you use these pause statements your emotions continue to circulate, and as this occurs, others around you will pick up on this vibration and inevitably calm down! So rather than tell everyone to leave you alone or answer haphazardly to get them off your back, develop the practice of using your pause statements. Pausing is far more powerful than rushing into a verbal response.

Here are some other things to keep in mind when developing this skill:

- Pausing is about allowing emotional flow, not preventing.

- Be sure to get adequate sleep and hydration. When you are tired or dehydrated, you are more likely to be quick in your responses.

- Unclench your back teeth before you speak. Tight jaws lead to unhinged speech.

- Give yourself transition time from one activity to the next. If you have a history of anxiety it is likely that you often put pressure on yourself or rush. Give yourself a couple of minutes of transition. With that said, be mindful you don't linger *too* long, as this can lead to procrastination.

SEEING THE "I AM" IN OTHERS

Seeing the "I am" in others means seeing others (especially ones who we are close to) as capable, resourceful human beings. Here is the thing: When it comes to processing emotions, everyone has this ability. Regardless of your background, intellectual ability, income, or history, you were born with the ability to feel and process your emotions. Your soul is already connected to how this works. The challenge is bringing it to the physical, human, everyday level. Most of us have not been taught how to do this, so now's the time!

Seeing the "I am" in others means seeing the good, the potential, and the beauty. The challenge is that without awareness that darn ego can get in the way and before you know it you have gone off on a tangent about all their faults. While you may really believe people are annoying you, there is more for you to know about this way of reacting. It wasn't until I was teaching about the "I am" presence in a C.L.E.A.N.S.E. yoga class that I had an "Aha!" moment that would help me break this unconscious habit. Here are two things you ought to know about the "I am" in others:

1. If someone is making you anxious or upsetting you, it is because you are disconnected from your "I am." See it as a reminder to hook up to your "I am" and practice a quick C.L.E.A.N.S.E. It is likely you are in reactivity.

2. Give others the time, space, and respect to hook up to their "I am." Know the signs of someone who is not in their "I am" presence. Rather than label them as difficult, immature, or selfish (which are all reactions), see them as someone who is not connected to the "I am." Have compassion because we've all been there. Trust their soul journey is exactly what they need to return to the "I am" state.

Signs of someone who is disconnected from the "I am" include:

- Little to no eye contact
- Scattered thoughts
- Shallow breathing (limited inhale)
- Physically tilted (e.g., not standing firmly or flat-footed on the earth)

If you encounter someone in this state, know that it is not your job to fix them. The best thing you can do is remain in your "I am" state so they have a reflection of how to return home.

THE FORGIVENESS FREQUENCY

Many people who read *Emotional Detox* asked me how I was able to genuinely forgive my husband for having an affair. I will tell you that it wasn't just about forgiving him; it was about loving myself enough to choose healing rather than reactivity. I knew that to react would mean to retraumatize and the consequences could go far beyond me. I knew that I could potentially pass on this way of reacting to my children and even my grandchildren, and I didn't want to risk that.

Living a life with ease means you are aware of your choices and you choose the path of least resistance. Living in the "I am" means you are choosing to love unconditionally. When you choose to feel rather than react, you are choosing to love. It is that simple. Ease is knowing you have the ability to convert any emotional frequency (anger, sadness, frustration, confusion, and all the emotions related to anxiety) into something new—forgiveness. You no longer need to cope, and that in itself is freeing.

RECAP

- Step 7 converts your "I allow" statement to your "I am" statement.
- Ease happens as you develop your "I am" presence.
- Notice the signs for when you are not in your "I am" presence.
- When you know when someone else is speaking outside of their "I am" presence, you learn to be less judgmental.
- The forgiveness frequency resides in the "I am."

CULTIVATE CALM

Emotions are what we were born with; reactivity is what we have learned and can unlearn.

PART 3
MANIFESTING JOY

AFTER YOU MOVE THROUGH THE C.L.E.A.N.S.E. PROCESS, YOU WILL FIND JOY. THE C.L.E.A.N.S.E. METHOD DOES MORE THAN REDUCE TOXICITY—IT IS ALSO A PRACTICE OF MANIFESTING! TO MANIFEST MEANS TO BE CLEAR, OBVIOUS, PALPABLE, DISTINCT, VISIBLE, AND UNMISTAKABLE IN HOW YOU DIRECT YOUR ENERGY. IT IS AN ETERNAL STATE OF CREATION. ACCORDING TO AUTHOR NEVILLE GODDARD IN *FEELING IS THE SECRET*, "SO IT IS TO CONSCIOUSNESS THAT WE MUST TURN IF WE WOULD DISCOVER THE SECRET OF CREATION." HERE IS WHAT I KNOW: YOUR THOUGHTS ARE POWERFUL—THEY IMPACT HOW YOU FEEL AND HOW YOU SEE THE WORLD. YOUR FEELINGS, HOWEVER, ARE HOW YOU CHANGE THE WORLD!

CHAPTER 9

SUSTAINING YOUR ANXIETY DETOX

"If we consider that the human body is a universe within itself, it is only natural to conclude that we carry within us all the elements."

—Masaru Emoto

By now, you're probably feeling hopeful. Your anxiety may have shifted from overwhelming to a state of clarity, or even been released completely. It is important to maintain a lifestyle that can help you sustain and enrich your anxiety detox and your emotional well-being as a whole. Consistency matters. The C.L.E.A.N.S.E. is not an on-again, off-again thing; you need to make it a part of your everyday life. "I don't have time" doesn't work as an excuse; that could well be a reaction to or symptom of anxiety. To help you avoid that excuse, here's a quick version of the C.L.E.A.N.S.E. that you can do while you're waiting for the water to boil for tea, while you're waiting to pick up your kids from school, or while you're standing in line at the store.

TAKING STEPS

Step 1: Clear Reactivity

- Three acupressure presses, neck stretch, standing or seated stretch, gaze toward floor.

Step 2: Look Inward

- How I feel in my body right now is _____ (*inhale... exhale...*).
- Being in my body right now is _____ (*inhale... exhale...*).
- Being still makes me feel _____ (*inhale...exhale...*).
- Having time makes me feel _____ (*inhale... exhale...*).
- Having no time makes me feel _____ (*inhale... exhale...*).
- When I care for myself it makes me feel _____ (*inhale...exhale...*).
- Not caring for myself makes me feel _____ (*inhale... exhale...*).

Step 3: Emit

- Hum three times (inhale, then exhale into a hum while closing your mouth).

Step 4: Activate Joy

- See it! Visualize what liberated and available looks like in nature.

Step 5: Nourish

- Feel it! Imagine the sensations associated with being liberated, free, and available.

Step 6: Surrender

- "I allow" statement: *I allow availability, I allow liberation, I allow freedom.*

Step 7: Ease

- "I am" statement: *I am availability, I am liberation, I am freedom...*

That's a straightforward version of C.L.E.A.N.S.E. you can do pretty much anytime and anyplace, but you will probably need additional support. If your body is quickly reverting back to low energy or those around you don't understand your new approach, anxiety is likely to take hold again. Following are some suggestions for sleep, food, supplements, exercises, and other resources to increase emotional flow, because it is difficult to manifest a life of inner peace and balance if you feel weak. Do all of these or as many as you can. Pay attention to how they affect your anxiety. How do you feel if you miss a day of vagal toning or "I am" statements?

GETTING A GOOD NIGHT'S SLEEP

Your emotions never go away. They are constant, whether you're awake or asleep—yes, they can even influence the quality of your rest and dreams. Sleep is designed to help release the stressors of the day, but as you've probably noticed, it can sometimes instead be a time when you get triggered! Let's face it, no one likes to get their sleep interrupted. Random noises, temperature changes, physical discomfort, as well as undigested emotions in general and anxiety in particular all impact how you sleep. Here are some tips for improving the quality of your sleep:

- **Try a weighted or gravity blanket.** These blankets are engineered to place between 7 percent and 10 percent of your body weight on you as you sleep. This extra pressure has been said to increase serotonin and melatonin levels, which are known to decrease anxiety. I've gotten some great feedback from people with anxiety who have used them. I first heard about them through one of my psychology students who reported her husband's snoring triggered her. The blanket helped her sleep through the night!

- **Limit blue light.** "Blue light" describes that light from the screens we stare at all day (and all night) long—computers, tablets, phones, and so on. Blue light is known to interfere with melatonin (the hormone that regulates sleep cycles) production. Turn off screens (particularly phones and computers) and keep them at a distance from your body for a minimum of one hour (ideally two hours) before bedtime. You might also want to invest in some blue light glasses because they can reduce eyestrain and headaches caused by blue light. My daughter is on her computer quite a bit and found some inexpensive, fashionable ones online.

- **Limit or avoid caffeine and sugary foods.** Individuals with anxiety are often sensitive to moderate to high amounts of caffeine and refined sugar. Curbing late-night eating habits allows your body to calm down before bed. Think about it: When you eat something, your body has to dedicate energy to digesting and processing your food, not on easing into sleep. Eating at least three hours before bedtime allows your body to detox the day's food *and* emotions.

- **Invest in blackout shades and white noise machines.** According to a study published on NeuroscienceNews.com, "Skin and liver cells appear to have their own circadian clock. Both the liver and skin respond to changes in light and maintain critical function independent of the brain's circadian rhythm." It turns out your liver, which is one of your main detox organs, is influenced by light! Investing in shades and white noise machines may help keep light low and disruptions to a minimum.

EXERCISE

I see it again and again with my clients—those who incorporate exercise into their lives tend to sleep better and experience better health overall. Exercise is more than a way to get a good night's rest, build muscle, or release pent-up energy. While many types of physical movement can be good for anxiety, there is growing evidence that resistance training can help you break the worry cycle. (This kind of resistance is good for you!) Resistance training typically involves resistance bands, free weights, weight machines, medicine balls, or your own body weight. For example, Plank Pose—where you hold a push-up position (with your arms extended) for a few counts or breaths—can be a form of resistance training. One of my personal favorites is squats. In fact, it is not unusual for me to "prescribe" squats to my clients and students who are learning the C.L.E.A.N.S.E. method.

INCORPORATING EXERCISE INTO YOUR DAY

If picking up weights does not appeal to you, there are many alternative ways to exercise besides resistance training. According to the Anxiety and Depression Association of America, regular exercise can help reduce symptoms of anxiety and depression. A brisk workout can help alleviate symptoms for hours and you'll see more effects if you exercise regularly. Here are some ways to get exercise without joining a gym:

- Take the stairs.
- Park a distance from where you are going and walk to your destination.
- Get a personal trainer or workout buddy to hold you accountable.
- Walk your dog.
- Plan exercise into your schedule as you would an appointment.
- Have a "some is better than none" attitude, but aim for at least half an hour of movement per day.
- Intensify what you already do. If you have been walking around your neighborhood for years, consider kicking it up a notch. Add some handheld weights, do a few lunges along the way, or end with some sit-ups.

PRACTICE YOGA

Like many of my students, I started taking yoga classes after years of struggling with anxiety and depression. At one point, I was on five different medications in one year. Often the transition from one medication to another was more stressful than the anxiety symptoms themselves. I decided I had nothing to lose by trying yoga.

Yoga is an ideal practice for those with anxiety. It comes in a variety of styles and difficulty levels, so you can choose one that's right for you. In addition, the National Institutes of Health has recognized it as a complementary form of medicine for both anxiety and depression. The following sequence of yoga poses can help ground and calm you.

SAMPLE OF A TEN-MINUTE GROUNDING EMOTIONAL FLOW ROUTINE

Exercise 1: Cat and Cow

Begin on your hands and knees in a tabletop position either on a yoga mat or a tightly woven carpet. Place your hands directly under your shoulders. On exhale, tuck your chin and tailbone, flexing your spine. Pull into your midsection where you do those three vagus nerve presses. As you round your spine, picture holding those three points for three to five seconds (you might find that you hold your breath here, so be mindful to breathe). Gradually inhale, and come naturally into your body (no force) as you tilt your head and tailbone upward, arching your spine. Repeat these movements three to five times in a row, inhaling as you lift your tailbone and heart, exhaling as you fold inward, holding those three points.

Exercise 2: Extended Child

After moving through your Cat and Cow Poses a few times, extend your arms forward, open your knees wide, and with your toes pointing together, sit back into your hips as you continue to reach your arms forward. Inhale, exhale. Remaining in this position, reach your arms to the left corner of your yoga mat as you open your waist on your right side. Inhale, exhale, then moving through center, reach to the opposite corner of your mat, stretching on your left side. Inhale and exhale. Be sure your breathing is in through the nose and out through the nose.

Exercise 3: Downward Dog

Draw your hands back directly under your shoulders on the floor in tabletop position. Then walk your hands about one or two hand lengths forward. With your feet roughly hip-width apart, tuck your toes and lift your knees slowly off the floor, extending the back of your legs back as you stretch and open the back of your body (hamstrings, calves) while lengthening your arms and spine. You will look like an inverted V. Breathe in this position. Inhale and exhale through your nose, pulling your navel toward your spine, pressing and releasing your vagus nerve, while strengthening your arms, legs, and spine. Hold for about three to five inhales and exhales. Then step forward to the top of your yoga mat and bow forward.

Exercise 4: Forward Fold

As you bow forward, know that you don't have to touch the floor. Bend your knees and touch your shins if necessary. As you continue to compress your vagus nerve (folding into your midsection), exhale and inhale. Allow your neck and shoulders to release and anchor them either on yoga blocks, the floor, or a piece of furniture (chair). You may also interlace your hands behind your back and lift your arms a bit away from your spine to stretch the shoulders. This allows you to open up your heart space. Exhale fully before you rise up on inhale.

Exercise 5: Rising Up to Hands on Heart

Slowly release your hands and arms and push into your heels and balls of your feet as you rise up to a standing position on inhale. Your arms will open and lift up to the ceiling or sky above you. Lift your arms up overhead, giving yourself a nice stretch before bringing your palms together in a prayer position over your head and then moving them down your center line on exhale, as they land right in front of your heart space. Take a moment to feel your breathing, and notice how processing your emotions is a way for you to begin your day. Feel how this grounds and centers you to the earth.

NOURISH YOURSELF

All that exercise is probably making you hungry! Let's think about the foods you're putting into your body and how they affect your emotional processing.

VITAMINS AND MINERALS

Many foods have an effect on anxiety levels, particularly ones that are high in magnesium. If you have a history of anxiety, it is important that you make sure you are getting a few essential vitamins and minerals. Dr. Mark Hyman, author of *Eat Fat, Get Thin*, calls magnesium the "relaxation mineral" and the antidote to stress. According to the National Institutes of Health, common signs of a magnesium deficiency include loss of appetite, nausea, vomiting, fatigue, and weakness. Some experts add insomnia and anxiety to that list.

So if you can only do one thing, this is it: Ask your doctor if it's all right for you to take magnesium (and calcium) on a regular basis. You can also increase your magnesium intake by eating foods like:

- Avocados
- Dark greens (kale, spinach)
- Legumes (chickpeas, other beans)
- Nuts (almonds, cashews)
- Seeds (pumpkin, flax, chia)

In addition, your doctor may encourage you to be sure you consume enough vitamins that include antioxidant properties to combat stress, such as vitamins A, B, C, D, and E. Some people are also finding L-theanine to be a great supplement for reducing symptoms of anxiety. You can also find this in a tea, but speak to a doctor or nutritionist about the dosage.

Increasing your vitamin intake through nutritious foods can ease anxiety by controlling blood sugar levels and improving your heart health. Some of these could also improve your overall circulation (and consequently oxygen levels), balancing your nervous system and emotional flow. Look for the following vitamins in the foods listed:

- **Vitamin A:** Sweet potatoes, spinach, broccoli
- **Vitamin B:** Grapefruit, eggs, dark leafy vegetables, nuts, seeds
- **Vitamin C:** Brussels sprouts, dark leafy vegetables, lemons
- **Vitamin D:** Fortified milk, orange juice, salmon, tuna
- **Vitamin E:** Sunflower oil, sunflower seeds, wheat germ, broccoli

PROBIOTICS AND PREBIOTICS

It's especially important that people who tend to be anxious consume enough probiotics. These are live bacteria and yeasts that are good for your digestive system. Often referred to as "good bacteria," they help you create a healthy gut. A recent study in the journal *Psychiatry Research* suggested that eating probiotic-rich foods such as pickles, sauerkraut, and kefir was linked to a lowering of social anxiety. Doctors will often encourage you to consume a probiotic while taking an antibiotic (or after) to restore the good bacteria that was killed off.

While selecting a good probiotic supplement may seem a little overwhelming, it is worth doing some research before making an investment. Probiotics generally are less effective when they are kept in warmer temperatures, so discuss proper storage and dosage with a health store or nutritionist.

If you prefer to eat them instead of taking a supplement, probiotics can also be found in foods such as:

- Yogurt
- Probiotic milk drinks
- Kombucha drinks
- Some soy products like tempeh and miso
- Pickles

While probiotics are designed to keep a healthy gut flowing (cleaning out the waste from the gut), think of prebiotics as food for probiotics. Since probiotics are live bacteria, they need to be fed to remain healthy in your system. Foods that are high in fiber often contain prebiotics. Here are some foods to introduce prebiotics in your system:

- Apples
- Asparagus
- Bananas
- Cocoa
- Flaxseed
- Oats

GETTING IN THE DIRT

Scientists have discovered that the less contact we have with dirt, the less resilient we become—and that by returning to the dirt, we can actually ward off anxiety disorders. It has been shown that a bacterium found in soil—*Mycobacterium vaccae*—interacts with immune cells to inhibit pathways that drive inflammation, therefore increasing resilience to stress. These findings were so impressive that some researchers are now working on a "stress vaccine." One recent study, published in the *Proceedings of the National Academy of Sciences* in 2017, showed that injections of *M. vaccae* prior to a stressful event could prevent a "PTSD-like" syndrome in mice, enabling them to fend off stress-induced colitis and making the animals act less anxious when stressed again later.

While this research is fascinating, my clients tell me it is not just being outdoors and in the soil (not to mention the sun) that makes them feel better, but also the sense of being connected to something greater in the universe—trees, ocean, and sky.

MORE WAYS TO INCREASE EMOTIONAL FLOW AND RELEASE ANXIETY

Following are more simple and easy ways you can boost emotional flow in your everyday life:

1. **Heating pad:** If you are someone who holds your emotions in your stomach area, consider putting a heating pad on your abdomen as you breathe in through your nose and out through your nose. Allow the gentle warmth to soften your muscles.

2. **Biomat:** A Biomat is an FDA-approved healing tool that uses ion technology. Often embedded with crystals, Biomats seem to reduce inflammation and improve circulation in your body. They tend to be a little pricier than regular heating pads, depending on the size.

3. **Infrared saunas and hot tubs:** Taking a sauna or soaking in a hot tub are both great ways to relax your muscles and breath. Some gyms offer saunas in their memberships. Since there is not much to do in a sauna, consider it a great opportunity to take yourself through the steps of the C.L.E.A.N.S.E.

4. **Sound therapy:** Sound therapy is a type of vibrational medicine. You can find sound therapy experiences and classes in multicultural centers and yoga studios. Some examples of sound therapy include drumming and crystal bowls. If you have never experienced this, it's worth checking out!

5. **Essential oils:** Nonsynthetic essential oils can be a wonderful way to soothe your nervous system. There is a variety of ways to use them: You can apply them on your skin, ingest them by placing a few drops in water, or diffuse them into the air. I recommend Doterra oils as they are all organic, smell amazing, and last!

6. **Massage, acupuncture, and reflexology:** These healing modalities are wonderful opportunities to increase emotional flow. If you want to know more about herbs, Chinese medicine, or supplements, try an acupuncturist as they often can provide a wealth of knowledge. Reflexology focuses on your feet, which have many acupressure points that connect to your organs. Massage will give you a whole-body approach. The key is to find someone you can let your guard down with, so you can sit back, enjoy, and trust.

7. **Spend time with animals:** Animals are a wonderful way to increase connection, slow down your heart rate, and lift your mood. If you can't have an animal in your life, consider volunteering at a shelter—the mere act of petting and spending time with animals can help increase your breathing capacity.

8. **Get out in nature:** Nature is vibration. If you are indoors a lot, working long hours, it is important to get out in the fresh air, preferably with sunshine, even if it is only ten to fifteen minutes a day. Try making small changes to your daily habits: eat your lunch outside, read your mail on your front steps, or walk to get some food

instead of using a food delivery app. You'll notice a big difference in the quality of your breath, thoughts, and ability to focus.

9. **Find time for connection:** While it might seem like work or school is high on your priority list, it is important to balance these obligations with time with friends and family. The busyness of life has a sneaky way of numbing you. You can get so accustomed to being alone that you forget how valuable emotional connection is. Consider joining a class, attending a church service, or volunteering in a group. Make time in your calendar for friends and family.

10. **Music:** Nothing increases emotional flow like the sound of music. My husband and I went to a live concert and floated in peaceful vibrations for days afterward. Notice how the type of music you are listening to impacts you. Does it increase your negative thoughts toward yourself and others or does it make you feel at ease, invigorated, and empowered? Be willing to explore different styles of music. One song you might want to check out is "Weightless" by Marconi Union as researchers have shown that listening to this song can alleviate anxiety!

11. **Download a C.L.E.A.N.S.E. audio:** Visit SheriannaBoyle.com to download guided C.L.E.A.N.S.E. meditations with binaural beats embedded in the background. (Binaural beats are known to increase blood flow and relaxation in the body.)

There you have it: a number of suggestions for sustaining your detox. While it might seem like a lot to consider, don't let it make you anxious! As you move through the practice, you will become naturally inclined to incorporate some of these strategies in your life. This is because they are aligned with love, self-care, compassion, and fostering inner and outer strength. The more you process your emotions, the less apt you will be to sacrifice some of these opportunities. Instead, you will relish these mini reinforcers, knowing each time that your efforts can enhance your detox and diminish the anxiety in your life.

RECAP

- Sustaining your detox is a natural progression with the C.L.E.A.N.S.E.
- Select the strategies that caught your attention. Go with what feels right rather than what you think is right.
- Exercise is a known remedy; it can soothe anxiety and build resiliency.
- Take in foods that enrich your circulatory, cardiovascular, and nervous systems with essential vitamins and minerals.
- Prioritize resources that support a healthy night's sleep.
- Balance exercise with mindful practices such as yoga.

CULTIVATE CALM

When you zoom in on what does not serve you—things like fear, doubt, and anxiety—you let in unhealthy habits and behaviors. Processed emotions allow you to zoom out so you can view your options.

CHAPTER 10
ENERGIZING THE GOOD!

"Shine like the whole universe is yours."

—Rumi

I had been up all night, tossing and turning on an air mattress. My daughters and I were playing hooky, taking a few days off from school to soak up the sun. It was unusual for me to take the girls out of school; however, that winter had been tough on us. I could tell the girls needed a good boost of vitamin D to lift their spirits.

My mother had invited us to Florida to stay with her friend. The place didn't have enough beds, so we took turns sharing the floor. When we accepted the invitation it sounded like a good idea, but then mom and her boyfriend had a tiff, and we discovered the house had no Internet so one of my daughters (who was homeschooled that year) couldn't access her classes.

Sleeping on the floor wasn't exactly what I'd had in mind for a vacation and I found myself wondering if we would have been better off staying at home. Just then I heard my girls laughing in the room next to me. This was medicine for my tension. The bond they share brought me a sense of calmness and peace. It was in that moment that I heard a clear yet distinct voice in my head: *Run it through the*

C.L.E.A.N.S.E. formula. That is when I learned how to energize the good—what this chapter offers you.

THE C.L.E.A.N.S.E. CAN ALSO ENHANCE HAPPINESS—BUT DETOX FIRST

You can use the C.L.E.A.N.S.E. with the intent to focus on releasing reactivity or as an opportunity to enhance the joy within you. The reality is that sometimes there is something you need to clear before you can focus your attention on manifesting. While focusing on the good and the positive is a great practice, I encourage you to slow down, because being a positive Pollyanna may be an unconscious strategy that you use to cover up and resist feelings rather than feel. An emotional detox encourages you to exchange faking for feeling, so be sure you've done that process first. Otherwise, you may unconsciously continue to expand what you don't want.

Here is the thing: You can conjure up all the positive thoughts you want, hang affirmations on your wall, and drink out of your beautiful Namaste mug—but until you feel all the emotions you are holding back or burying, you will never truly be able to experience the raw, pure energy those words, ideas, and dreams have to offer.

If you have been struggling with anxiety, it is likely that your ability to focus on the good is not well developed. Depending on your level of anxiety, how long your focus on the good lasts can range from a few seconds to hours. For example, you may smile or hear yourself say something like, "Ahh, that is nice." Maybe you see a picture of a kitten that temporarily softens your heart; however, because you are so used to operating in fear, you find that feeling fades quickly.

When it comes to manifesting joy, love, abundance, and all that other good stuff, I suggest taking a moment to slow down. Honor what is showing up inside you rather than covering it up with coping mechanisms. Manifesting happens within the joy frequency. Just like it may take time to get to know a new school, part of town, or routine, give yourself some time to get to know joy. In this chapter I offer a deeper understanding of joy. Before heading there, let's take a moment and apply that mindset to the C.L.E.A.N.S.E. method.

TAKING STEPS

Step 1: Clear Reactivity

- Three acupressure presses (one inch above the navel), and neck stretches on both sides with a five-second hold on each side.

Step 2: Look Inward

- How I feel in my body right now is _____ (*inhale... exhale...*).
- Listening to my daughters' laughter makes me feel _____ (*inhale...exhale...*).
- And when I hear their laughter it makes me feel _____ (*inhale...exhale...*).
- Sitting in the sun makes me feel _____ (*inhale... exhale...*).
- Swimming in the pool makes me feel _____ (*inhale...exhale...*).

Step 3: Emit

- Hum three times.

Step 4: Activate Joy

- See it! Visualize joy.

Step 5: Nourish

- Feel it! Experience joy sensations (make it come alive through senses in your mind).

Step 6: Surrender

- "I allow" statement: *I allow joy, I allow laughter, I allow movement, I allow nourishment, I allow connection...*

Step 7: Ease

- "I am" statement: *I am joy, I am laughter, I am movement, I am nourishment, I am connection...*

MANIFESTATION GUIDELINES

While you may be tempted to use the C.L.E.A.N.S.E. formula primarily for manifesting, slow down. This is a process, not a product. When I teach the method, I teach it in two parts. Level 1 demonstrates how to use the formula in daily life and dig into the subconscious in a deeper way, as well as how you might sabotage the process. Once you get the hang of it and have strengthened your emotional flow, then you can move to Level 2, which focuses on manifesting.

Think of your emotions as a stream of sensations. What may start out as a trickle will eventually move into a deep river. You don't want to attempt to manifest from only a trickle—this may kick in some old fear-based habits. To support you on this path, here are some guidelines to consider:

- **Let the process unfold naturally.** While you may be tempted to use the formula as a means for changing your life, be mindful that this could be a reaction on your part. Should this occur, choose to detach from results by running it through the formula.

- **Take time to receive the lessons.** As you C.L.E.A.N.S.E. reactivity, you will receive tremendous insight and learnings about yourself and the world around you. This insight is like gold. Take the time to fully receive this wisdom and knowledge.

- **You can't screw this up!** When using the formula, you can't screw things up. Choosing to move through the steps will never hurt you. You might get a little off track here and there, but the universe knows your intentions and will always support you.

- **Practice reflecting on the good.** Notice how you look back on your day. Do you focus on what you accomplished or the joy that showed up in your life that day? Strengthen your awareness of joy. Simple things like sharing a meal, chitchatting with a stranger, or receiving a hug from a loved one should be atop your list of things you reflect on.

- **Write in a gratitude journal.** Many people find it helpful to keep a journal of the things they are grateful for. You may even refer to them as daily appreciations or daily joy. Writing things down on a regular basis can help you develop clear intentions.

- **Do what you love.** Becoming someone who manifests means letting yourself (and others) do what you love. If you love eating, eat with joy; if you love biking, bike with joy; if you love watching movies, do it with joy.

- **Notice what you are drawn to.** Some people may be unsure of what they love, so notice what you are drawn to. I love healthy food, but I don't always feel comfortable cooking. I was drawn to a business card once and I kept it in my car's visor for months before I made the call to sign up for a class. Now I cook with more joy.

- **Let go of outcome.** While you may be accustomed to controlling or predicting the future, the C.L.E.A.N.S.E. will help you loosen these tendencies. Here is the thing: The universe has a much broader view than you. Trust the direction you are in. If you are making comparisons, run it through the formula, as that is a reaction.

- **Notice what comes your way.** Anxious people tend to assume everything is a bad sign. Let yourself be curious and surprised by what and who comes your way. For example, someone may connect you to a support group, refer a client, or give you the exact piece of advice you needed to hear that day. Soak up that joy!

- **Supercharge through sleep.** Your physical body needs sleep, but your manifesting potential never sleeps. If you are an anxious sleeper—meaning, all your worries and doubts come up to the surface to be revisited when you lie down for the night—consider doing your C.L.E.A.N.S.E. practice before you go to bed. As you doze off, give the universe permission to help you create your dreams. Let your higher self and spiritual guides give you a loving hand in creating your vision.

REMEMBER: ANXIETY DEPLETES YOUR POWER

When you focus on what you want (anxiety mode) rather than tuning in to what you have (emotions and their energy), you deplete your manifesting power. It is kind of like drinking a smoothie from a leaky cup, never getting to the sensation of feeling full. Overthinking and processing deplete your energy. So, to strengthen your ability to create, focus on your inner first and allow the steps in the formula to guide you into your visualizations. Here is an example of purifying an attachment to wanting and then manifesting abundance through the C.L.E.A.N.S.E.

TAKING STEPS

Step 1: <u>C</u>lear Reactivity

- Three acupressure presses, neck stretch on both sides, and add side gaze.

Step 2: <u>L</u>ook Inward

- How I feel in my body right now is _____ (*inhale... exhale...*).

- Wanting makes me feel _____ (*inhale...exhale...*).
- When I need more it makes me feel _____ (*inhale... exhale...*).
- When I want something it makes me feel _____ (*inhale...exhale...*).
- Wishing for something makes me feel _____ (*inhale...exhale...*).

Step 3: Emit

- Hum three times.

Step 4: Activate Joy

- Visualize images of gathering, collecting, conceiving, and producing.

Step 5: Nourish

- Feel it in your body!

Step 6: Surrender

- "I allow" statement: *I allow gathering, I allow collecting, I allow producing, I allow maintaining...*

Step 7: Ease

- "I am" statement: *I am producing, I am gathering, I am creating...*

Feels good, doesn't it? Manifesting in this way is so incredibly nourishing and compassionate to your body. It supports the idea that you already have everything you desire; you just need to allow it to exist within you.

GETTING TO KNOW JOY

Noticing the good means noticing joy, which one might say is the opposite of living in anxious reactivity. Depending on how you were raised and what you were or weren't exposed to, joy can sometimes be misinterpreted as conditional. If you were raised in an authoritarian environment and often heard things like "Do it because I said so," then you may be a little tentative or reluctant to experience joy. On the other hand, if you were raised in an environment with little to no structure, where "Do whatever the heck you want, when you want" was the rule, you may view anyone who tries to give you some constructive feedback as squashing your joy.

Here is what I know: Joy is not one extreme or the other. It is everything yet at the same time it is dependent on nothing. Joy happens the moment you notice a slight twinge of motion; this is because joy is internal energy. Once you have noticed and experienced it, you have already altered your path. Joy is a shifter, but it does so by aligning you with your higher self rather than taking you off course through reactivity.

When you are quick to label, reason, interpret, or control, you are overriding the joy frequency. No worries; it is still there—joy doesn't disappear. Unlike happiness, it isn't dependent on you doing, having, or being good. Joy doesn't come to you, it *is* you. And when you truly get this, manifesting becomes not a tool but a birthright. (Go back and take another look at the table in C.L.E.A.N.S.E. Step 4: Activate Joy to review the differences between happiness and joy.)

Here are some of my favorite ways to encounter joy:

- Compassion
- Feeling your feet on the earth
- Holding hands or hugging
- Kindness
- Laughter and smiling

- Nature
- Sunrises and sunsets
- Water
- Wildlife and animals

You can use my suggestions or come up with your own list!

THE LANGUAGE OF JOY

As you can see, joy takes you from a space of effort (resistance) to non-effort (flow). As you strengthen your manifestation muscle, it is important to be aware of how you might extinguish the early moments of joy. I find one of the ways this can happen is through the choice of language you use to communicate with yourself or others. Yes, how you express and communicate impacts your manifesting potential.

Words are vibration, and if you use them without awareness, they can be a sign that you are in a trigger. This is why it is so important to understand the difference between a trigger (reactivity) and healing before manifesting.

The emotional detox process helps you choose to consciously notice and reframe what you say. Not because what you are doing is wrong, bad, or insulting but rather because it may snuff out joy. Here are some examples of reactive language followed by language connected to joy:

REACTIVE LANGUAGE	JOY LANGUAGE
I try...	I choose...
Maybe...	Yes...
I think...	I am...
What was, before, last time, in the past...	What is, today, now...
I should...	I notice...
I don't understand...	I wonder...

What I have learned is that words such as "maybe" and "I think" carry a frequency of uncertainty and doubt. They basically save space for fear. While no one is perfect, reframing how you speak takes time and compassion. It is your awareness and decisions to pause and reframe yourself that make a difference. In many ways, your choice to notice and choose a new way of speaking may be more powerful than the words themselves. After all, joy is what happens when you utilize your free will for the greater good.

EXPECT AMAZING THINGS

Because the C.L.E.A.N.S.E. method teaches you how to feel, visualize, and allow higher frequencies (emotions) into your life, don't be surprised if you (like I did) start manifesting ideas, things, situations, seeds you planted long ago. This is because when you are not attached to outcome or extinguishing the joy frequency (by holding on to anxiety), manifesting new responses, opportunities, and attitude shifts can happen!

For years, I dreamed of teaching at renowned retreat centers all over the world. I wondered how to get my work into *Yoga Journal* and other respected outlets such as *Psychology Today* and the National Alliance on Mental Illness (NAMI). As an adjunct psychology professor, I would daydream about other methods for treating anxiety. It wasn't until I started to practice the C.L.E.A.N.S.E. method that all of this effortlessly came into fruition. Since then, I have helped clients shift from struggle to joy, tap into their higher potential, and use the formula as a way to manifest their dreams, connections, and healthier lifestyles. You too will see things shift as you use this method. For example, you may find yourself feeling more confident or able to be more centered and present in your life. These can also be signs of manifesting something new.

RECAP

- Anxiety interferes with your manifesting power.
- Replace faking with feeling.
- Slow down and integrate the manifesting guidelines.
- Joy is the manifesting frequency.
- Getting to know joy will maximize your manifesting muscle!

CULTIVATE CALM

While anxiety may have diminished your dreams, your emotions will revitalize them.

AFTERWORD:
THE EMOTIONAL DETOX
MOVEMENT

About eight years ago, I had the honor of sitting in a sacred circle with a Native American chief. I thought I was there to learn more about his leadership, his responsibilities, and how he earned a title of the highest respect, but I learned so much more. Although he spoke very little, his few words were powerful, and his presence made one of the greatest impacts on my life. What he taught me was the power of being an observer.

The emotional detox movement is about taking responsibility for your own inner resistance. Sure, what you feel matters; however, processing what you feel matters more. I believe what is happening on the outside—conflict, war, famine, disease—is a collective result of a long history of non-feeling. Stepping into the emotional detox movement is a way to turn the tide. It's an opportunity to introduce and pass on higher wisdom to future generations.

While anxiety may have contributed to the imbalances in your life, know that your struggles will not be wasted. In fact, the larger the struggle, the more energy you have to contribute to this planet. Your choice to step into the observational role will have a tremendous ripple effect. While it may be easy to get sidetracked by the noisy people standing on their soapboxes, yelling and screaming, I say keep your eyes on the quiet ones, the observers, because they are the most powerful, as are you.

The emotional detox movement encourages you to look beyond the label of your feelings, detach from the meaning of the words, and allow yourself to feel the vibration. Teach children not just what their feelings are but how to process them. See their wiggly bodies as their most natural instinct for processing and downloading this priceless energy. Discipline your mind with the steps, and have faith rather than attachment to outcome. The emotional detox movement allows you to grow beyond what is right or wrong, instead seeing everything as an opportunity to C.L.E.A.N.S.E.

Thank you from the bottom of my heart for opening yours and letting your emotions shine through. Until next time...be free.

With joy,
Sherianna

EMOTIONAL DETOX TERMINOLOGY

Anxiety:
An emotion looking to be digested but can't be because it is being resisted.

Coping Mechanisms:
Ways you have learned to manage your emotions.

Emotions:
Neuropeptides, chemical signals, molecules, and atoms in motion. Different emotions have different vibrational frequencies. The more uplifting the emotion the higher the rate of movement in your body (frequency).

Emotional Detox:
A seven-step mindful process for digesting your emotions.

Energy:
Molecules and atoms in motion that provide you with strength and vitality.

Joy:
A state of expansion.

Manifesting:
Bringing something forth in your physical life through the process of digesting your emotions.

Meridians:
The energy pathways or channels that run through your body and circulate your life-force energy.

Overprocessing:
The way in which you over-think and analyze your feelings. Worrying is an example of overprocessing.

Pattern:
The vibrational frequency of your emotions held at a certain rate. For example, you may have a pattern of feeling guilty for taking care of yourself.

Processing:

Taking emotions through the natural process of being transformed into a higher state of awareness.

Raw:

When you experience your sensations as is, without trying to control them.

Reactivity:

How you make the uncomfortable comfortable. Typically, reactivity is how you go to your brain (thoughts) to manage or resist an emotion.

Sensation:

The way in which emotions are experienced in the human body.

Trigger:

A charge of discomfort in the body that may be an indication that there is an undigested emotion related to an unhealed wound in your body. Triggers are memories of buried emotions brought forth through current events.

Undigested Emotions:

Show up as triggers, bodily tension. They can also contribute to symptoms of anxiety and other diseases.

Vibration:

The electromagnetic energy of your emotions running at a certain rate (frequency) through your body.

C.L.E.A.N.S.E. SAMPLES

DAILY C.L.E.A.N.S.E. BASIC ROUTINE

STEP 1: CLEAR REACTIVITY

- Three presses, neck stretches.

STEP 2: LOOK INWARD

- How I feel in my body right now is _____ (*inhale... exhale...*).
- Being in my body right now makes me feel _____ (*inhale...exhale...*).
- Tuning in to my body now makes me feel _____ (*inhale...exhale...*).

STEP 3: EMIT

- Hum three times.

STEP 4: ACTIVATE JOY

- See it! Visualize images that represent feeling serene, peaceful, calm, grounded, and centered.

STEP 5: NOURISH

- Feel it! Sense, smell, and tune in to sensations of calm.

STEP 6: SURRENDER

- "I allow" statement: *I allow calm, I allow peace, I allow centeredness…*

STEP 7: EASE

- "I am" statement: *I am calm, I am peace, I am centered, I am free…*

GENERAL ANXIETY C.L.E.A.N.S.E. SAMPLE

STEP 1: CLEAR REACTIVITY

- Three presses, neck stretches, cat/cow stretch.

STEP 2: LOOK INWARD

- How I feel in my body right now is _____ (*inhale... exhale...*).
- Breathing makes me feel _____ (*inhale...exhale...*).
- And when I breathe it makes me feel _____ (*inhale...exhale...*).
- Having tension (e.g., in my neck) makes me feel _____ (*inhale...exhale...*).
- And when my neck and shoulders are tight it makes me feel _____ (*inhale...exhale...*).

STEP 3: EMIT

- Hum three times.

STEP 4: ACTIVATE JOY

- See it! Visualize images in nature that represent relaxation, calmness, and confidence.

STEP 5: NOURISH

- Feel it! Feel the sensations from these images in your body; for example, the feeling of a calm, confident tree or sunrise.

STEP 6: SURRENDER

- "I allow" statement: *I allow calm, I allow confident, I allow relaxation…*

STEP 7: EASE

- "I am" statement: *I am calm, I am confident, I am relaxed, I am free…*

PANIC ATTACK C.L.E.A.N.S.E. SAMPLE

STEP 1: CLEAR REACTIVITY

- Three vagus nerve presses, neck stretches, and three squats. (Stand up with your feet parallel and squat down *slowly* on the count of three. Stand up and repeat two more times.) Do three more vagus nerve presses. Loosen your body by rolling your shoulders and neck around.

STEP 2: LOOK INWARD

- Doing these three presses makes me feel _____ (*inhale...exhale...*).
- When I stretch my neck it makes me feel _____ (*inhale...exhale...*).
- Squatting down now makes me feel _____ (*inhale... exhale...*).

STEP 3: EMIT

- Hum three times.

STEP 4: ACTIVATE JOY

- See it! Visualize images of calmness, peace, and strength.

STEP 5: NOURISH

- Feel it! Imagine what calm, peace, and strength feel like. Perhaps think of a beautiful bird spreading its wings on top of a tree.

STEP 6: SURRENDER

- "I allow" statement: *I allow calm, I allow strength, I allow peace...*

STEP 7: EASE

- "I am" statement: *I am calm, I am strength, I am peace, I am free...*

SOCIAL MEDIA C.L.E.A.N.S.E. SAMPLE

STEP 1: CLEAR REACTIVITY

- Three presses, neck stretches, cat/cow stretch.

STEP 2: LOOK INWARD

- How I feel in my body right now is _____ (*inhale... exhale...*).
- Looking at social media makes me feel _____ (*inhale...exhale...*).
- When I surf social media it makes me feel _____ (*inhale...exhale...*).
- Not looking on social media makes me feel _____ (*inhale...exhale...*).
- Posting on social media makes me feel _____ (*inhale...exhale...*).
- Not posting on social media makes me feel _____ (*inhale...exhale...*).

STEP 3: EMIT

- Hum three times.

STEP 4: ACTIVATE JOY

- See it! Visualize images in nature of security, confidence, and calm.

STEP 5: NOURISH

- Feel it! Imagine what these images would feel like sensation-wise in your body.

STEP 6: SURRENDER

- "I allow" statement: *I allow security, I allow confidence, I allow peaceful, I allow calm...*

STEP 7: EASE

- "I am" statement: *I am secure, I am confident, I am peaceful, I am calm, I am free...*

BIBLIOGRAPHY

Andrews, Linda Wasmer. "How Strength Training Helps Keep Anxiety at Bay." *Psychology Today.* March 29, 2017. Accessed June 30, 2019. www.psychologytoday.com/us/blog/minding-the-body/201703/how-strength-training-helps-keep-anxiety-bay.

Anxiety and Depression Association of America. "Exercise for Stress and Anxiety." Anxiety and Depression Association of America. Accessed June 30, 2019. https://adaa.org/living-with-anxiety/managing-anxiety/exercise-stress-and-anxiety.

Anxiety and Depression Association of America. "Understand the Facts." Anxiety and Depression Association of America. Accessed June 30, 2019. https://adaa.org/understanding-anxiety.

Cleveland Clinic. "Vital Signs." Cleveland Clinic. January 23, 2019. Accessed July 1, 2019. https://my.clevelandclinic.org/health/articles/10881-vital-signs.

Digital Communications Division. "What Are the Five Major Types of Anxiety Disorders?" US Department of Health & Human Services. February 12, 2014. Accessed June 30, 2019. www.hhs.gov/answers/mental-health-and-substance-abuse/what-are-the-five-major-types-of-anxiety-disorders/index.html.

Emoto, Masaru. *The Hidden Messages in Water.* Translated by David A. Thayne. New York: Atria Books, 2005.

Fader, Sarah. "Social Media Obsession and Anxiety." Anxiety and Depression Association of America. November 2018. Accessed June 30, 2019. https://adaa.org/social-media-obsession.

Felman, Adam. "What Causes Anxiety?" *Medical News Today.* October 25, 2018. Accessed June 30, 2019. www.medicalnewstoday.com/articles/323456.php.

Fox, Andrew S., Jonathan A. Oler, Rasmus M. Birn, Alexander J. Shackman, Andrew L. Alexander, and Ned H. Kalin. "Functional Connectivity Within the Primate Extended Amygdala Is Heritable and Associated with Early-Life Anxious Temperament." *The Journal of Neuroscience* 38, no. 35 (2018): 7,611–621. www.jneurosci.org/content/38/35/7611.

Freedman, Joshua. "The Physics of Emotion: Dr. Candace Pert on the Mind Body Connection and Feeling Go(o)d." Six Seconds. January 26, 2007. Accessed June 30, 2019. www.6seconds.org/2007/01/26/the-physics-of-emotion-candace-pert-on-feeling-good/.

Gaia staff. "Mysteries of the Human Heart." Gaia. Accessed June 30, 2019. www.gaia.com/article/mysteries-of-the-human-heart.

Goddard, Neville. *Feeling Is the Secret.* Whitefish, MT: Kessinger Publishing LLC, 2010.

Goddard, Neville. *Neville Goddard: The Complete Reader.* Audio Enlightenment, 2013.

Goldman, Jonathan, and Andi Goldman. *The Humming Effect: Sound Healing for Health and Happiness.* Rochester, VT: Healing Arts Press, 2017.

Hamilton, Jon. "Researchers Discover 'Anxiety Cells' in the Brain." *Morning Edition.* January 31, 2018. Accessed June 30, 2019. www.npr.org/sections/health-shots/2018/01/31/582112597/researchers-discover-anxiety-cells-in-the-brain.

Harvard Medical School. "Generalized Anxiety Disorder." *Harvard Mental Health Letter.* Harvard Health Publishing. May 17, 2019. Accessed June 30, 2019. www.health.harvard.edu/newsletter_article/generalized-anxiety-disorder.

Hawkins, David R. *Power vs. Force: The Hidden Determinants of Human Behavior.* Carlsbad, CA: Hay House, 2014.

Hyman, Mark. "What's the Deal with Magnesium?" *The New Potato.* April 2017. Accessed June 30, 2019. www.thenewpotato.com/2017/04/05/why-is-magnesium-important.

Koshland Jr., Daniel E. "The Molecule of the Year." *Science* 258, no. 5,090 (December 18, 1992): 1,861. Accessed June 30, 2019. https://science.sciencemag.org/content/258/5090/1861.

Loyd, Alexander. "Cellular Memory Healing: How to Clear Limiting Beliefs and Emotional Wounds at the Cellular Level." *Conscious Lifestyle Magazine.* Accessed June 30, 2019. www.consciouslifestylemag.com/cellular-memory-healing-clearing/.

Meah, Asad. "The Law of Vibration from Bob Proctor." *Awaken the Greatness Within.* Accessed June 30, 2019. www.awakenthegreatnesswithin.com/the-law-of-vibration-from-bob-proctor/.

Miller, Marjorie S. "Emotions Like Anger and Sadness May Cause Pain As Well As Being a Result of It." *Medical Xpress.* September 10, 2018. Accessed June 30, 2019. https://medicalxpress.com/news/2018-09-emotions-anger-sadness-pain-result.html.

Na, Hae-Ran, Eun-Ho Kang, Jae-Hon Lee, and Bum-Hee Yu. "The Genetic Basis of Panic Disorder." *Journal of Korean Medical Science* 26, no. 6 (May 18, 2011): 701–10. https://jkms.org/DOIx.php?id=10.3346/jkms.2011.26.6.701.

Naidoo, Uma. "Nutritional Strategies to Ease Anxiety." *Harvard Health Blog.* April 13, 2016. Accessed June 30, 2019. www.health.harvard.edu/blog/nutritional-strategies-to-ease-anxiety-201604139441.

National Institutes of Health—Office of Dietary Supplements. "Magnesium: Fact Sheet for Health Professionals." US Department of Health & Human Services. September 26, 2018. Accessed July 1, 2019. https://ods.od.nih.gov/factsheets/Magnesium-HealthProfessional/.

Neuroscience News staff. "Body Parts Respond to Day and Night Independently from Brain." Neuroscience News. May 30, 2019. Accessed June 30, 2019. https://neurosciencenews.com/body-parts-circadian-rhythm-14129/.

Neuroscience News staff. "Healthy Fat Hidden in Dirt May Fend Off Anxiety Disorders." Neuroscience News. May 29, 2019. Accessed June 30, 2019. https://neurosciencenews.com/dirt-fat-anxiety-14108/.

Pedersen, Traci. "Achieve More by Resisting Less: Understanding the Spiritual Law of Least Effort." Spirituality & Health. June 24, 2015. Accessed June 30, 2019. https://spiritualityhealth.com/blogs/spirituality-health/2015/06/24/traci-pedersen-achieve-more-resisting-less-understanding#.

Perry, Philip. "How We Breathe Affects Our Thoughts and Emotions, Northwestern Researchers Find." Big Think. January 4, 2017. Accessed June 30, 2019. https://bigthink.com/philip-perry/how-we-breathe-effects-our-thoughts-and-feelings-northwestern-neuroscientists-find.

Pert, Candace B. Molecules of Emotion: The Science Behind Mind-Body Medicine. New York: Touchstone, 1999.

Proctor, Bob, and Sandra Gallagher. The Art of Living. New York: TarcherPerigee, 2015.

Rydall, Derek. "The Secret Language of Desire." DerekRydall.com. January 23, 2014. Accessed June 30, 2019. https://derekrydall.com/the-secret-language-of-desire/.

Shohani, Masoumeh, Gholamreza Badfar, Marzieh Parizad Nasirkandy, Sattar Kaikhavani, Shoboo Rahmati, Yaghoob Modmeli, Ali Soleymani, and Milad Azami. "The Effect of Yoga on Stress, Anxiety, and Depression in Women." International Journal of Preventive Medicine 9, no. 1 (February 21, 2018): 21. www.ijpvmjournal.net/article.asp?issn=2008-7802;year=2018;volume=9;issue=1;spage=21;epage=21;aulast=Shohani.

Squires, Sally. "Molecules of Emotion." The Washington Post. August 21, 1985. Accessed June 30, 2019. www.washingtonpost.com/archive/lifestyle/wellness/1985/08/21/molecules-of-emotion/b9357aaa-a702-425c-a832-0dd3a182b2c3.

Strickland, Justin C., and Mark A. Smith. "The Anxiolytic Effects of Resistance Exercise." *Frontiers in Psychology* 5 (July 10, 2014): 753. www.frontiersin.org/articles/10.3389/fpsyg.2014.00753/full.

Thomas, Scot. "Alcohol and Drug Abuse Statistics." American Addiction Centers. June 13, 2019. Accessed July 1, 2019. https://americanaddictioncenters.org/rehab-guide/addiction-statistics.

Vann, Madeline R. "Is Anxiety Hereditary?" Everyday Health. August 24, 2015. Accessed June 30, 2019. www.everydayhealth.com/news/is-anxiety-hereditary/.

Vergara, Tess. "Awaken Possibilities: Embrace the Feminine Power." Open Heart Mind Coaching. January 2014. Accessed June 30, 2019. http://openheartmindcoaching.com/wp-content/uploads/2014/01/Awaken-Femininity-Lesson-2-Plan.pdf.

Wagner, Kathryn Drury. "The Science Behind Healing with Sound." UPLIFT. January 17, 2017. Accessed June 30, 2019. https://upliftconnect.com/science-behind-healing-sound/.

Wanderly, Natasha. "How to Know You Have Fully Forgiven: An Ultimate Guide to Forgiveness." *Mindvalley Blog*. November 24, 2018. Accessed June 30, 2019. https://blog.mindvalley.com/forgiven/.

Wei, Marlynn. "Can Probiotics Help Reduce Anxiety?" *Psychology Today*. September 28, 2018. Accessed June 30, 2019. www.psychologytoday.com/us/blog/urban-survival/201809/can-probiotics-help-reduce-anxiety.

Williamson, Marianne. *A Return to Love: Reflections on the Principles of a Course in Miracles*. New York: HarperOne, 1996.

Wong, Cathy. "Meridians in Acupuncture and Chinese Medicine." *Verywell Health*. May 6, 2019. Accessed June 30, 2019. www.verywellhealth.com/what-are-meridians-88946.

Yeh, James K., John F. Aloia, Halina M. Semla, and Shang Y. Chen. "Influence of Injected Caffeine on the Metabolism of Calcium and the Retention and Excretion of Sodium, Potassium, Phosphorus, Magnesium, Zinc and Copper in Rats." *The Journal of Nutrition* 116, no. 2 (February 1986): 273–80. Accessed June 30, 2019. https://academic.oup.com/jn/article-abstract/116/2/273/4763137.

Zhu, Shaotong, Colleen M. Noviello, Jinfeng Teng, Richard M. Walsh Jr., Jeong Joo Kim, and Ryan E. Hibbs. "Structure of a Human Synaptic GABA$_A$ Receptor." *Nature* 559, no. 7,712 (June 27, 2018): 67–72. www.nature.com/articles/s41586-018-0255-3.

STAY CONNECTED TO SHERIANNA BOYLE

Emotional Detox for Anxiety workshops, Emotional Detox Level 1 and Level 2 trainings, Emotional Detox coaching, and online classes can be found at SheriannaBoyle.com, which is also where you'll find my *Emotional Detox* podcast! Or visit me on:

- *Facebook*: www.facebook.com/SheriannaBoyle/
- *Twitter*: @SheriannaBoyle
- *Instagram*: @sherianna.boyle

Other books by Sherianna Boyle, available at bookstores, libraries, and online:

Emotional Detox: 7 Steps to Release Toxicity and Energize Joy

The Four Gifts of Anxiety: Embrace the Power of Your Anxiety and Transform Your Life

Choosing Love

Mantras Made Easy: Mantras for Happiness, Peace, Prosperity, and More

The Conscious Parent's Guide to Childhood Anxiety: A Mindful Approach for Helping Your Child Become Calm, Resilient, and Secure

The Everything® Parent's Guide to Overcoming Childhood Anxiety: Professional Advice to Help Your Child Feel Confident, Resilient, and Secure

Powered by Me® for Educators Pre-K to 12: The True Force Behind All Classroom Strategies, Higher Teaching Potential and Student Progress

INDEX

Fear, letting go, 61–63
Food additives, 38–39
Food benefits, 39–40
Forgiveness, 188–91
Free will, 82, 89–90, 143, 166, 218

Generalized anxiety disorder, 20
Genetic makeup, 32–34
Goals, setting, 103–6, 109–12, 114
Goddard, Neville, 173, 193
"Going raw," 51–53, 91–102, 223
Goldman, Andi, 140
Goldman, Jonathan, 140
Gratitude, 164–65, 168, 213

Happiness, 65, 148, 152–53, 210–19.
  See also Joy
Hawkins, David R., 99
Healing, 16, 53–54, 135–46
Heart chakra, 151–52
Holland, Anthony, 140
Hum, 135–53
Human connections, 40–42, 111–12,
  155, 161–62
Human time, 155–56
Hyman, Dr. Mark, 202

"I allow" statements, 169–84, 192,
  197, 212, 215, 225–29
"I am" statements, 181–92, 212, 215,
  225–29
"I feel" statements, 129–31, 135–36,
  148, 171
Immune system, 64, 141, 205
Inflammation, reducing, 51, 58–59,
  118, 131, 205
Inner space, healing, 53–54, 143–44
Intentions, setting, 103–6, 109–12,
  213
Inward, looking, 127–36
Isolation, 41–42, 77

Joy
  activating, 147–56

bliss and, 108–9, 128
definition of, 222
energizing, 99, 209–19
happiness and, 65, 148, 152–53,
  210–19
language of, 217–19
manifesting, 193–219
noticing, 216–17
sustaining, 195–208
visualizing, 147–52, 156–59, 176,
  184, 196, 211–19
Judgments, making, 60–62, 96–97

Letting go
  of fear, 61–63
  healing and, 143
  of old ways, 52, 157, 172
  of outcome, 213
  of resistance, 77, 186–87
  surrendering and, 169–80
Listening skills, 166–68
Loneliness, 31, 41–42
Look Inward step, 7, 127–36

Manifesting
  definition of, 222
  expectations for, 218–19
  guidelines for, 212–14
  joy, 193–219
  supercharging, 65–66
Mantras, 135, 137, 140–43, 146
Medications, 51, 200
Meditation
  brainwave entrainment and, 139
  for calmness, 16, 78
  guided meditations, 207
  observation and, 87–88
  visualization and, 33, 122–26, 151
Meridians, 58–59, 84, 222
Mind chatter, 7, 25, 74–75, 89–90,
  94–96
Misinterpretations, 97–99, 216
Müller, George, 67

Named One of the Ten Life-Changing Self-Help Books Every Woman Should Read in 2019 by *Parade* Magazine

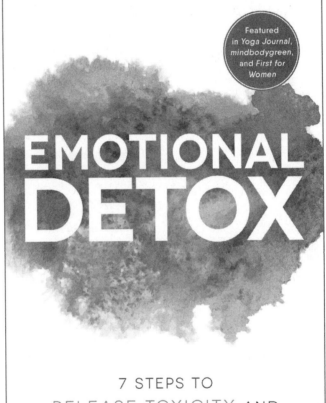

Featured in *Yoga Journal*, mindbodygreen, and *First for Women*

EMOTIONAL DETOX

7 STEPS TO RELEASE TOXICITY AND ENERGIZE JOY

SHERIANNA BOYLE, MED, CAGS

PICK UP OR DOWNLOAD YOUR COPY TODAY!